To my wife Diana,
who always lets me go
to the mountains...

SCRAMBLES
in the Canadian Rockies

ALAN KANE

ROCKY MOUNTAIN BOOKS - CALGARY

Cover: Kris Thorsteinsson near the summit of Pika Peak in the Skoki region of Lake Louise. To his left is the connecting ridge to Mt. Richardson.

Title Page: Interesting scrambling on Mt. Burstall's east ridge.

All photos by the author except where noted otherwise.

Published by Rocky Mountain Books
106 Wimbledon Crescent,
Calgary, Alberta T3C 3J1

The publisher wishes to acknowledge the assistance
of the Alberta Foundation for the Arts and Alberta
Culture in the production of this book

*Printed and bound in Singapore by
Kyodo Printing Co. (S'pore) Pte. Ltd.
Separations and halftones by
United Graphic Services, Calgary*

Canadian Cataloguing in Publication Data

Kane, Alan, 1954-
   Scrambles in the Canadian Rockies

   Includes index.
   ISBN 0-921102-07-0

   1. Hiking--Rocky Mountains, Canadian (B.C.
and Alta.)--Guidebooks.* 2. Rocky Mountains,
Canadian (B.C. and Alta.)--Guide-books.* I.
Title.
FC219.K35 1992   917.1104'4   C92-091210-9
F1090.K35 1992

CONTENTS

Scrambling Areas

DISCLAIMER

There are inherent risks in scrambling in the mountains. Although the author has alerted readers to situations and locations where particular caution is to be exercised, conditions on any of the routes may change at any time. Scramblers use this book entirely at their own risk and the author disclaims any liability for any injuries or other damage which may be sustained by anyone scrambling up any of the peaks described in this book. The scrambler's attention is directed to the section entitled **"Words of Warning"** on **page 9**.

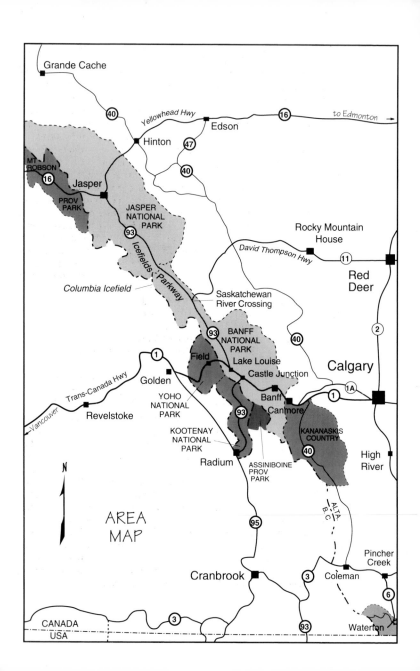

AREA MAP

PREFACE

I could have used this book about ten years ago. An ardent hiker and backpacker, I wanted a little more challenge; better views. The only easy ascents I was sure of were Mount Allan, Heart Mountain and Mount Rundle. So began an apprenticeship involving rock-climbing and mountaineering courses followed by research in various books and journals and finally, many excursions to many different peaks. Some routes didn't require the use of a rope. A close friend, Kris Thorsteinsson, believed that other people would like to know of such routes, and so I began documenting them in detail.

Without his sharing the original idea and his companionship on the majority of the ascents, this book would not have been completed. To all who furnished information over the years, written or verbal, I thank you very much, especially my fellow climbers in The Alpine Club of Canada, Calgary Section. They have often related their escapades, successful or otherwise, with little prodding. Needless to say, volumes such as The Rocky Mountains of Canada South have been invaluable.

To those who find errors in this book, please let me know. As roads and trail heads change, so do access routes. Inaccuracies are therefore bound to occur, but with ongoing rapport among users, this can hopefully be minimized in future. To all who use the information contained between these covers, enjoy. With any luck, you will avoid some of the pitfalls which I experienced. Also, know a good scramble?
Send suggestions to:
Alan Kane
920 - 36 Street N.W.
Calgary, Alberta T2N 3A8

ACKNOWLEDGMENTS

There is much more to writing a mountain guidebook than simply going out and climbing some mountains. Even once the text was written, I found the end was still nowhere in sight, and without the efforts of several other people, this book would not have been completed. Tony and Gillean Daffern did the layout, supplied photos, helped with proofreading and offered suggestions along the way; Kris Thorsteinsson gave me free reign over his thousands of slides; also, he, Gary Fauland and Andy Riggs made suggestions and helped in proof-reading. I owe thanks to Wendy Shanahan, Donna Pletz and Juliette deChambre of Canadian Parks Service, and to the following people whose pictures I have used: David M. Baird, Don Beers, Reg Bonney, Clive Cordery, Bruno Engler, Leon Kubbernus, Glenn Naylor and Canadian Parks Service. I must also thank those who searched their oft-sizeable photo collections but whose pictures don't appear here for one reason or another. Lastly, my wife Diana deserves a special mention. It can't be easy living with a mountain fanatic.

INTRODUCTION

Of the profusion of guide books covering the Canadian Rockies, none specifically targets the realm of easy non-technical mountain ascents, otherwise referred to as scrambles. This volume attempts to cover a small portion of that ground. Hikers and backpackers may find these ascents a logical and perhaps more challenging step beyond day hikes and backcountry camping. At the other end of the spectrum, the book should provide climbers with ammunition for solo and training outings without the bother of doing any legwork beforehand.

An attempt has been made to address questions regarding degree of difficulty, route of approach, identity, height, distance and length of ascent time, and special equipment that may be needed. Some would suggest that with all this information supplied, the element of adventure has been removed. Not so. Rapidly changing weather and poor quality of rock will spice up many of these outings regardless. Similarly, despite the detail there are sure to be instances where route descriptions will be misinterpreted. This too can result in more adventure than expected. Finally, those feeling strongly enough can ignore the detailed information — the choice is theirs. The foremost idea of this book has been to supply enough information to prevent nasty surprises, and to up the success rate for all enthusiasts.

Peaks described cover a broad scale from famous and eye-catching to obscure. Difficulties range from little more than a stiff walk up a big hill, to ascents involving scrambling up small cliff bands, traversing narrow ridges or moving up moderately steep snow slopes. Specialized equipment such as an ice-axe, crampons and perhaps a length of climbing rope could be required on some routes. Often the route recounted is not the only one that will "go", but it is one that has proved itself. Most of the scrambles can be done in a single day, thereby eliminating the need for heavy overnight packs. The majority of outings use existing trails on the walk in; nobody actually enjoys bushwhacking.

While adequate information concerning trail heads and approaches has been included, a more complete description of most access routes may be found in two popular books: Kananaskis Country Trail Guide by Gillean Daffern, and The Canadian Rockies Trail Guide by Brian Patton and Bart Robinson. Both are widely available.

Environmental Considerations

There are few places in the world as pristine as the Canadian Rockies. Every time you venture off the trail to short-cut a switchback or tramp across a meadow, some amount of damage, although slight, occurs. Think of this before you choose to blaze your own way while everybody else follows the path. Conversely, because you see nobody else on the route is no reason to leave your pop can on the peak or your Kleenex on the trail. Many people use the mountain areas regularly and the usage is increasing steadily. Please do not diminish the experience for the next party by your thoughtless actions. At the present time, besides a cairn and register, most summits bear little evidence of visitors. It would be nice if it stayed that way.

One final note: In the past, persons have removed entire summit registers as proof of their accomplishments. Please don't do this. Take a picture, take a stone, but let others record their names and read the booklet too. Enough preaching — well, almost.

Words of Warning

All the reading in the world is no substitute for experience, and it is not the intention of the author to convey anything to the contrary. Undertaking trips mentioned in this volume is a potentially hazardous activity and should be treated as such. Particular phrases contained within route descriptions could be misconstrued to suggest a lack of danger and difficulty. This is not so. Participants are advised to proceed with caution and select a route within their abilities. Those lacking requisite skills and experience would benefit from enrolling in a course through a recognized Alpine School or a registered mountain guide. Clubs such as The Alpine Club of Canada are tailored specifically to mountain enthusiasts and are well worth joining. They conduct courses and group outings regularly.

In pursuit of your objectives, do not allow enthusiasm to overshadow good judgement; keep the goal in perspective. It should be the aspiration of all scramblers to develop and hone their mountains skills continually, so as to rely less and less on the skill of companions. As you do, your level of confidence will rise accordingly. Persons following any advice or suggestions contained within these pages do so entirely at their own risk.

Alpine Schools

Canadian School of Mountaineering
629 - 10 Street
PO Box 723
Canmore, AB T0L 0M0
Ph (403) 678-4234

Yamnuska Inc.
1316 Railway Avenue
PO Box 1920
Canmore, AB T0L 0M0
Ph (403) 678-4164

Peter Amann Guiding
PO Box 1495
Jasper, AB T0E 1E0
Ph (403) 852-3237

Jasper Climbing School
PO Box 452
Jasper, AB T0E 1E0
Ph (403) 852-3964

Useful Guidebooks

"The Canadian Rockies Trail Guide" by Brian Patton & Bart Robinson.

"Kananaskis Country Trail Guide" by Gillean Daffern.

"Hiking Lake Louise" by Mike Potter.

"The Wonder of Yoho" by Don Beers.

"The World of Lake Louise" by Don Beers.

"Hiking Historic Crowsnest Pass" by Jane Ross & William Tracy.

"Backcountry Biking in the Canadian Rockies" by Gerhardt Lepp.

"Selected Alpine Climbs in the Canadian Rockies" by Sean Dougherty.

SCRAMBLING IN THE CANADIAN ROCKIES

The scrambling season varies from year to year and range to range. An old-timer once said that a year in the Rockies is ten months of winter and two months of poor sleddin'. This is simply not so. It just takes more searching during those two months. On a more serious note, south and west-facing slopes in the Front Ranges get into shape by May or June. North and east-facing slopes take a few weeks longer. As you approach the Continental Divide and the Main Ranges further west, it is often mid-July before any amount of snow-free scrambling can be undertaken. Some years an extended or "Indian" summer will stretch the season right into November — preferable to baking on a scree slope in July.

Registration

Voluntary registration is available in National and Provincial Parks at warden offices as well as at info centres in Kananaskis Country. It is wise to let somebody know of your plans should you decide to go alone. Be sure to register in if you registered out. You are legally required to do this. Failure to do so can result in a needless search, which in turn will be costly. Authorities can hold you personally liable for the entire expense.

Mountain Bikes

Mountain bike use is tightly controlled on National Park trails, and is limited mainly to fire roads such as Redearth Creek. In Kananaskis Country, there are far fewer restrictions, and except for interpretive trails, most are open to biking.

Times and Directions

Ascent time is given based on the assumption that you are in good physical condition through a regular regimen of biking, jogging, hiking or similar activity. Monthly walks do not count. As a guideline, 300 m (1000') elevation gain per hour is a reasonable pace.
Descent time is not given, but is typically half to two-thirds your ascent time.

Directions are referenced relative to the direction of travel.

Maps indicated are the 1:50,000 scale National Topographic System series. Six digit references to grid co-ordinates are frequently mentioned. An explanation of this locating method may be found on the border of each map. Maps included in this book are intended only to show the positions of specific mountains in relation to major highways.

Grading

Simple descriptions of easy, moderate and difficult have been adopted and, where appropriate, information such as the degree of exposure (potential fall distance) may be included. This system does not relate directly to existing systems of grading climbs. Suffice to say difficult is less than 5.4 on the Yosemite Decimal Scale. A better explanation might be:

> **Easy** — mostly hiking, minimal use of hands, little exposure if any. e.g. Mount Bourgeau.

Moderate — frequent use of hand-holds, perhaps some exposure, some route-finding required. e.g. Cascade Mountain, Big Sister.

Difficult — much use of handholds required, portions may be quite exposed and steeper. Rock may be smooth and down-sloping, and loose. Route-finding skills very helpful to recognize most practical way for specific sections. A length of climbing rope could also prove useful. e.g. Mount Stephen, Dolomite Peak.

Routes normally become significantly harder when conditions are wet, snowy or icy. Keep in mind that **unroped scrambling is one of the most potentially dangerous mountain activities**, particularly where exposure (fall distance) is appreciable. This fact is well supported by accident statistics.

Be aware that down-climbing is more difficult than climbing up. If the scrambling unnerves you going up, consider an alternate route, since climbing back down the same place will be worse. If in doubt, perhaps a different and easier objective would be more to your liking.

Equipment

Sturdy leather half or three-quarter shank boots are ideal for these ascents. Runners and ultra-light boots give too little ankle support, especially on talus slopes which comprise a good part of many routes. They also wear out quickly on this same terrain. Plastic mountaineering boots are hot, clumsy and don't last long on scree. Ski-poles are of much help on scree slopes, particularly new easily-stowed collapsible models. Europeans have been using these for years. Certain routes may warrant the use of an ice-axe and crampons depending on the amount of snow remaining. Many scramblers carry an ice-axe as a matter of course. If you aren't familiar with the use of these items, have someone show you. Better yet, enroll in a basic one or two day snow and ice course through various clubs and mountain schools. Consider carrying a helmet for steeper routes or if a crowd is expected.

Clothing

Plenty of clothing that can be worn in layers is the norm. Raincoat, windpants, toque, wool gloves, cap, pile or fleece jacket, wool or synthetic shirt, polypropylene undershirt and calf-height gaiters are suggested. Cotton is clammy when it gets wet, and should be avoided if cool temperatures are anticipated.

Miscellaneous Items

Good sunblock cream, glacier glasses or sunglasses that eliminate ultra-violet rays, lip cream, compass, water-bottle, large handkerchief and toilet paper distinguish the prepared scrambler from the novice. A small but appropriately stocked first-aid kit, commercial or home-made, should also be considered. A camera is a useful item. Besides recording your exploits for posterity it serves as a legitimate excuse for periodic stops.

HAZARDS

Mountains are inherently hazardous. Increased demand for adventure is revealing a disturbing trend among the populace. Many individuals are not willing to bear responsibility for their own actions in case of an accident. For these souls, golfing or similar safe activities are suggested. If you won't accept the risk, don't go. If you do accept the risks, an indication of what to expect follows.

Weather

Weather in the mountains is capricious and unpredictable. Rain, snow and thunderstorms can and do occur throughout much of the season, sometimes running the full gamut during a single afternoon. Temperatures regularly dip below freezing at night, while hot afternoon sun on a scree slope is enough to cause heatstroke. Weather forecasting for the Canadian Rockies is anything but an exact science. Expect surprises.

Rockfall

The Canadian Rockies are notorious for loose rock as is evidenced by massive scree and talus slopes that provide simple routes to the top. Handholds can unexpectedly pull out in your hand, but often a good thump with the palm will indicate whether or not a hold is trustworthy. Good rock becomes a term that must be taken in context, since often it lies under varying amounts of rubble, particularly on those much-appreciated ledges. If you have an aversion to loose terrain, steep or otherwise, you are unlikely to find many scrambles in the entire Canadian Rockies to your liking.

Stonefall on frozen mountain faces increases as the sun warms them. The resultant melting releases frozen rocks which can then plummet of their own accord. Gullies often act as funnels for such debris. The most likely source of rockfall may well originate with the party itself, although mountain sheep and goats have been known to knock down rubble once they perceive a threat below. Since it may be next to impossible to avoid dislodging some projectiles, it is in your own interest to avoid scrambling below other groups. Climbing in The Rockies without a helmet is considered foolhardy, and, though not usually needed on easier routes, some steeper and more technical scrambles could also warrant head protection. For these same reasons, think twice about going with a crowd unless the route is a basic scree-plod.

Avalanches

Snow avalanches are unlikely to be a serious menace on most open south and west-facing ridge routes as the snow melts or slides off early in the season. Gullies can be another matter. They should be carefully assessed as to avalanche potential beforehand. Firm snow can alleviate the drudgery of toiling up loose scree while providing the opportunity to glissade the return, but once the summer sun strikes these south and westerly slopes they rapidly become mush. This dictates an early start to elude the possibility of a wet snow slide on steeper faces. Wet snow avalanches occur most frequently in spring and early summer, and although they move slowly compared to winter powder snow and slab avalanches, they quickly set up like concrete.

Wildlife

Apart from bears, few animals present a threat. To minimize a chance bear encounter, carrying a noisemaker such as a bell is recommended. When camping, hang anything that smells even remotely edible a good 4 m up a tree or between two trees away from camp. Keep your camp clean and follow these suggestions to reduce the possibility of bear problems. Watch for droppings along the trail. You don't have to be an expert to differentiate between types of bear scat: If it contains a bell, suspect a grizzly. Just kidding.

Insects

Little critters which bother backcountry folks in the Rockies are chiefly horseflies, mosquitoes, and, during spring and early summer, wood ticks. There are several insect repellents available for mosquitoes. Some people swear by an Avon product, Skin So Soft. Its effectiveness wanes quickly, but your skin will love you for it. Ticks hate DEET, the active ingredient in most good bug lotions so if you don't mind the smell this may help.

Although everyone enjoys exercising the right to bare arms, wearing long-sleeved shirts, gaiters, pants, a hat, and checking often for these pests is probably as effective as a repellant. Ticks prefer the hairy areas of the body, which can make finding and removing them by yourself an experience. They carry Rocky Mountain Spotted Fever only in extremely rare cases. So far, experts are dubious about these same ticks transmitting Lyme disease, but if you feel unwell after being bit, it's a good idea to notify your doctor. The disease progresses rapidly.

Water

Giardiasis or "Beaver Fever" is a protozoan parasite which contaminates surface water and brings misery to anyone unfortunate enough to ingest it. Symptoms can take up to 15 days to manifest themselves and may include persistent diarrhea, cramps, weakness and loss of appetite. Some authorities would have you believe it runs rampant in the mountains. Personal experience and that of numerous acquaintances over several years suggests otherwise, as all have regularly drunk from streams and suffered no apparent ill-effects. This situation could change in years to come.

Common sense decrees one should refrain from drinking out of valley bottom streams, where faecal contamination by beavers and dogs is a strong possibility. Simply stated, giardia hazard is inversely proportional to elevation. If everyone maintains good toilet practices (burying it), and keeps their mutt out of the backwoods, water quality should remain acceptable. When in doubt, 10 minutes of boiling will do the trick. So will 4-8 drops per litre of tincture of iodine. Shake well and let stand 10 minutes.

WATERTON LAKES

Mount Galwey	2348 m	moderate	p. 16
Mount Crandell	2378 m	moderate	p. 18
Mount Blakiston	2920 m	moderate	p. 22
Mount Lineham	2728 m	easy	p. 24

Waterton Lakes National Park, the most southerly area of any covered in this book, is the Canadian section of International Peace Park. Glacier National Park on the U.S. side forms the southern portion. Situated at the extreme south-west corner of Alberta, this small (518 sq km) preserve is popular for its backpacking and hiking trails, of which there are many. Little in the way of serious mountaineering is to be found, due in large part to the looseness of the rock. Although some of the oldest sedimentary rock in all the Rockies exists here, the quality has not improved with age. There are a few good scrambles though, as well as some scree-heap walk-ups, such as Mount Alderson.

Perhaps more than anywhere else, Waterton Park is known for its winds. The gales seem to blow regularly, much to the delight of board-sailers on nearby lakes, and to the dismay of campers in the town campground. For many, this is the first demonstration that all tents are not created equal. Chinooks — warm, westerly winds prevalent from about December to April — also occur here. When combined with a somewhat lower snowfall, these conditions guarantee a longer than average scrambling season than areas farther north. If snow persists in Bow Valley and Kananaskis, Waterton may be the place to go for a weekend.

Though close to prairie, Waterton Park displays much evidence of past glaciation, with surrounding mountain walls sculpted into craggy sentinels. Many of the peaks appear as high, castellated towers of horizontally-bedded layers, but rock quality is generally poor. The colourful red and green outcrops so widespread are argillite — a term applied to rocks known as "mudstones". As one might suspect, such rock does not make for trustworthy handholds. Waterton Parks policy does not encourage technical climbing in the area due to this unreliable rock. For anyone attempting ascents other than those covered in this volume, steep faces should be treated with suspicion.

Access to Waterton Park is via Highway 6 from Pincher Creek, some 48 km north, and by Highway 5 connecting to Cardston, 45 km east. Chief Mountain Highway , which provides access from the United States is open in summer only. Within the Park is 16 km-long Akamina Highway beginning right at the townsite and 15 km-long Red Rock Canyon Road beginning a few kilometres to the north-east.

Facilities Waterton is very much a summer-oriented tourist operation, and from mid-May to October you should be able to find almost everything you need in the way of groceries,

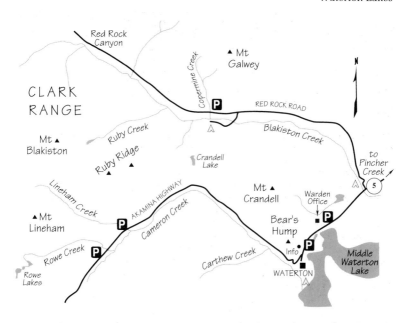

service stations, restaurants, camping and hiking supplies and souvenirs. Everything is comfortably close within the townsite. Since it is a National Park, a valid National Parks visitor permit is required and can be purchased at the Park entrance. When you've done enough tramping about, scenic boat and horse rides are popular, and mountain bikes can also be rented.

Accommodation There are several campgrounds in the area, both inside and immediately outside Park boundaries. Showers are available at the townsite campground — the windiest site of any. Drying your hair should be no problem here. Motels, chalets and so forth are also available for those fed up with roughing it.

Information An Information Centre is located just before the centre of town across from the Prince of Wales Hotel, a historic Waterton landmark.

Wardens Even if you do not plan on registering, Wardens are happy to provide detailed information on routes, conditions, weather or anything you might want to know — within reason, of course! The Warden Office/Maintenance Compound is located just past the golf course on the right-hand side as you approach the townsite.

MOUNT GALWEY 2348 m

Difficulty A moderate/difficult scramble via south-west aspect
Ascent time 2-4 hours
Height Gain 960 m
Map 82 H/4 Waterton Lakes

Despite its small stature, an intriguing shape elevates Mount Galwey to more than just another roadside attraction. It is easy to pick out on the way to Red Rock Canyon. Rolling, verdant hills lead the wandering eye to stark, dry slopes crowned by a blunt arrowhead summit. The very shape begs investigation. Judging by register entries, many do just that — repeatedly.

Follow Red Rock Canyon Road for 7.8 km to Coppermine Creek picnic area.

Beginning at Coppermine Creek picnic area, follow what begins as a promising trail up undulating hills on the right-hand side of the stream. Stay well above the drainage to avoid a narrow, canyon-like section, and tramp along the rounded crest of the open ridge leading directly towards Mount Galwey. En route you pass a sizeable outcrop of rich red rock — red argillite of the Appekunny Formation. Angle left above the headwaters of the right-hand (south) fork of Coppermine Creek and continue working diagonally up and left circling the peak in a clockwise direction. This places you above a scree basin feeding the north fork of Coppermine Creek. Galwey's defences are weaker on this side.

Although the strata is decidedly down-sloping and rubbly as you plod around, persevere. Ledges become more horizontal as you reach the steeper stuff. Until it topples one day, a key landmark to watch for is a rock pinnacle capped by a much larger rock etched against the skyline. The shape resembles a mushroom. Some distance below this feature, a gully breaks the first steep rockband, steering you towards vertical blocks stained yellow with lichen. Ascend this gully. The chute narrows as you climb, and the blackish band — possibly quartzite — is fabulously solid. Too bad there is so little of it. Emerging upon a level platform, possibilities look few. Now you are higher than the point where a north-trending ridge abuts against the summit mass. You search vainly to your left for some break in the next cliff band. The view southward, past a rock "wing" projecting airily over the abyss only suggests serious exposure. However, it is this direction — straight ahead — that you continue. There is, in fact, no sheer drop but a sloping scree bay a few metres below. Traverse into it on small but solid ledges (crux). Now you are onto a more southerly aspect and nearing the top. Just off to the right, a rectangular window through an otherwise solid rock wall frames the view of prairies lying east. The way is obvious now. Follow the path of least resistance and scramble easily up to the flat summit.

Mount Galwey is named for Lieutenant Galwey, an astronomer with the BBC — not a radio station, in this case, but the British Boundary Commission.

Mt. Galwey from Coppermine Creek picnic area.

Prairie view through window near the summit.

MOUNT CRANDELL 2378 m

Difficulty Difficult with exposure via
Bear's Hump; moderate via Tick Ridge
Ascent time 2-4 hours
Height Gain 1040 m
Map 82 H/4 Waterton Lakes

Mount Crandell offers an opportunity to
scramble up a small summit on the very
doorstep of Waterton townsite. Three
different routes discussed in decreasing
order of difficulty can be readily combined to effect a traverse. In spite of a
radio repeater squatting on top the ascent is worth doing. Try from May on.

Depending on choice of route, access
either via Bear's Hump behind Waterton
Park Tourist Information Booth, or from
Waterton Park Warden Office, 5 km
north-east of the townsite.

*Mt. Crandell sits on the doorstep of Waterton
townsite. Approximate location of route from Bear's
Hump is shown. B Bear's Hump, T "Tick" ridge,
D descent*

Bear's Hump approach

Most demanding of the three described
routes is an ascent from Bear's Hump.
Beginning at the Tourist Information
Booth, follow the signed path which
fizzles to scratchings of an animal trail
shortly beyond Bear's Hump. Continue
directly up to the first steep wall. Sud-

Photo: David M. Baird

denly, things take on a more serious nature. For the next several hundred vertical feet, the least problematic way is to keep traversing left on ledges — many are partly treed — and search for weaknesses which allow you to ascend successive cliffbands.

The rock is solid but at times quite smooth. It is pointless to even attempt to describe an exact line; innumerable possibilities exist and choice depends largely on your level of commitment and skill (or luck!) at route-finding. Well-beaten trails in strategic spots are made by street-wise Bighorn Sheep who eventually tire of panhandling around town and escape here to get away from it all. It is usually worthwhile following paths that appear — these beasts are no fools. Despite superb climbing skills they often choose the easiest way.

Bear's Hump approach. A foreshortened view from the townsite.

After surmounting several rockbands, you emerge onto easier terrain within a huge bowl which acts as a collecting basin for waterfalls cascading to Akamina Highway. The skyline ridge on your right is a fairly narrow and challenging continuation of the ascent. Coincidentally, the "Tick" ridge route beginning close to the Warden Office (described next) intersects at about this point.

You can either scramble on the crest of the airy cockscomb or, if desired, wander and scramble along the foot of it on the left (west) side. This avoids the most tenuous bits. At some point though, you must regain the crest of this ridge as continuing to traverse alongside becomes too demanding. By then difficulties on the ridge will be much less daunting. Challenges diminish as you approach the top.

Due to the degree of route-finding required on the lower and middle sections, this ascent route would present significant challenges on descent. Similarly, until you top out there is no quick way off. Any gullies end in cliffs. The usual **descent** route is described on page 21.

"Tick" Ridge

An easier line of ascent starts close to the Park Warden Office/ Maintenance Compound. It is obvious and readily examined from the highway. It should be noted, however, that Waterton Park Wardens do not encourage use of this route despite its straightforward nature, and with just cause. Any dislodged rocks can fall directly into the Parks' Compound and cause serious damage. If you do choose this option, for your continuing good health, use the utmost care not to knock anything down. Falling objects (and bodies!) are not appreciated.

Walk uphill through the grassy meadow just north of the Warden's parking lot, aiming for the bottom of the big south-east-facing drainage gully where a stream flows. Tick ridge which rises diagonally to the left offers a no-nonsense line of ascent. Only minor detours into trees are required to overcome a couple of steeper steps before it joins up with the cockscomb described under the ascent from Bear's Hump.

"Tick" Ridge route on Mt. Crandell.

Cockscomb ridge on the upper part of the mountain...breathe deep! Summit is at right.

Mt. Crandell as seen from the road. T Tick Ridge, D descent route.

In **descent**, the easiest and quickest way off utilizes open slopes on the right (north) side of the south-east facing drainage gully which emerges slightly north of the Warden Office.

From the summit drop down through larch forest, angling left as you lose elevation. Keep left of the main drainage system which becomes better defined as you descend. Do not follow the creek down into narrow confines. Instead, stay well above it on open slopes to the left, going overtop a jutting promontory — easily seen from the road, then scramble down the path of least resistance, aiming roughly for the stream's exit point into the meadow below. As a finale, flail through bush alongside the creek for the last few minutes. Total descent time may be less than one hour.

Mount Crandell is named for Calgary businessman, Edward Henry Crandell, who had been drawn to the short-lived oil seep "Discovery Well" on Cameron Creek, identified today by a roadside monument.

21

MOUNT BLAKISTON 2920 m

Difficulty Moderate scrambling
via south slopes
Ascent time 3-5 hours
Height Gain 1350 m
Map 82 G/1 Sage Creek

Ease of both approach and ascent has established Waterton's highest point as a most popular scramble. Entries in the register describe a diversity of ascent routes and traverses with adjacent, less lofty, peaks. Some require roped climbing. The normal (scramblers) way follows up south-facing scree slopes punctuated by brief rock steps which staunchly attempt to maintain a presence amid mounting debris. Try from June on.

From Waterton townsite, follow Akamina Highway for 9.4 km to Lineham Lakes trailhead (unsigned) on the north side of the road. NOTE: Upper part of route is visible from Rowe Lakes trailhead, 1.3 km farther down highway.

Follow the wide, well-graded Lineham Lakes trail as it switchbacks onto luxuriant grassy slopes before seeking the depths of sombre forest. In one hour you suddenly escape shady coniferous timber and are greeted with a first view of Lineham Creek plunging dramatically over a vertical headwall. More importantly though, this clearing you have entered is the run-out zone of a massive avalanche gully off Mount Blakiston, and serves as the usual line of ascent.

A search for difficulties on the route suggests few, and terrain appears to be sloped at a relatively laid-back angle. Left of the actual summit, dark castellated cliffs have eroded completely to allow unrestricted passage to the ridge. Most rock steps between appear to be surmountable in perhaps as little as a single bound. By comparison, for those who may have studied this objective from the top of nearby Mount Lineham, this same ascent route appears discouragingly long and the angle unpleasantly steep — too steep for scree to sit on. In actual fact, the truth lies somewhere between these extremes. The scree does stay put, but only until stepped on.

Most parties keep to the right side of the gully on ascent. Stunted evergreens, defying sweeping yearly slides, huddle precariously in the lee of the first bluffs you approach. In June, it is sometimes feasible to go up consolidated remnants of climax avalanches. However, for this you will definitely need an ice-axe. Eventually the angle begins to get a little uncomfortable, and if snowy, you will probably prefer the talus instead.

Although Mount Lineham obstructs much scenery initially, step by tedious step the peaks in nearby Glacier Park and British Columbia emerge on the horizon. As you draw closer to impending cliffs you may notice a couloir directly under the summit. It begins at the first weakness to the left of the vicious east face drop-off and offers a more interesting finish. Exasperatingly loose scree impedes your efforts until you reach a band of locally widespread red rock that supports the black summit cliffs. If you ascend the couloir, steep but wonderfully firm rock flaunting fluorescent yellow lichen quickly eases and ushers you to the top. It is unfortunate that on an ascent measured in hundreds of metres, this bit, the best and only real scrambling, is measured in mere metres.

Little distance separates prairie from peak in Waterton, and the eye is free to roam between eroded summits and rolling grasslands to the east. Cameron Lake is visible to the south and beyond, mightier mountains — residents of United States — reach skyward. Barely visible is the broad Flathead Basin further west.

The fastest **descent** logically avoids summit cliffs by wandering just a short way down the ridge. Lower down, there can be good glissading early in the season, although some stretches are just too steep while others end abruptly on rock. It goes without saying — well, almost without saying — that you carry an ice-axe and know how to properly self-arrest. Park Wardens are quick to recount a past incident on this mountain where someone glissaded into rocks and broke a bone.

One other hazard for persons ascending snow slopes is the very real possibility of breaking through areas which have been weakened by water flowing over underlying rock bands.

Mt. Blakiston ascent route viewed from Mt. Lineham — not nearly as steep as it looks!

Mount Blakiston is named for Lieutenant Thomas Blakiston, explorer, ornithologist and member of the Palliser Expedition. After a falling out with Palliser, he was sent packing, which he did, visiting China, Australia, New Zealand and England before finally settling in United States.

MOUNT LINEHAM 2728 m

Difficulty An easy ascent
Ascent time 2.5-4 hours
Height Gain 1110 m
Map 82 G/1 Sage Creek

Mount Lineham's south aspect presents little more than a walk; indeed, many hikers trudge to the top by the markedly more circuitous Tamarack trail/west ridge approach. The top gives an excellent view of the normal route on Mount Blakiston, and in early June, south-facing snow slopes make for a good glissade and an ideal place to practice ice-axe self-arrest techniques. Try from June on.

From Waterton townsite, follow Akamina Highway 10.4 km to the Rowe Lakes/Tamarack trailhead on the north side of the road.

From the parking area, follow the Rowe Lakes trail for about one hour to the first avalanche slope. Besides thrashing through greenery at the start of this slope, the route is so easy it shouldn't require the use of hands at all. Speaking of greenery, although this particular patch is small, avalanche areas like this provide much of a grizzly bears' diet, including glacier lilies and false helle-bore. If you don't have a bell or a noisy friend along, it might be the ideal time to perfect those vocal stylings. Above the avalanche vegetation, the route is a walk up scree or snow slopes to the summit.

From the top, you may notice Chief Mountain, the cone-shaped peak rising above numerous scree slopes to the south-east. From a geological standpoint, Chief Mountain is of special interest. It is the front of what was once a massive 6.5 km-thick wall of rock extending to Mount Kidd in Kananaskis

Ascent route. These gentle south slopes can make for a good glissade in these conditions!

Photo: Gillean Daffern   *The scenic west ridge of Mt. Lineham offers no difficulties.*

hundreds of kilometres north. It was pushed north-east as a largely continuous sheet, travelling a horizontal distance of some 70 km or so. Geologists, anxious to find faults, did not let this event slip by unnoticed. The Lewis Thrust was soon identified and named, and though similar incidents have occurred elsewhere in the world, few rival this one for magnitude. Normally, the oldest rock would lie at the bottom of the heap, but when such faulting occurs, older rock gets pushed up onto younger rock — a decidedly unnatural sequence. As a result of this aberrant act 80 million years ago, part of what should have been British Columbia now rests in Alberta.

As an **alternative descent route**, a scenic variation can be incorporated using a portion of Tamarack hiking trail. This loop offers a spectacular view of Lineham Lakes which you can't obtain by the direct south slope route. From the summit, wander down the west ridge being careful not to let unexpected Waterton winds push you over the escarpment on your right! Once you gain Tamarack Trail, follow it back, past the Rowe Lakes junction and ultimately to your vehicle. Distance from Lineham Ridge/ Tamarack Trail intersection back to the parking area is 8.5 km. While this option is without difficulty, it does add distance and time. You'll feel a little more like you've done an honest days' work should you decide to complete this loop.

Mount Lineham is named for John Lineham, a transplanted Englishman and a notable Alberta pioneer, largely credited with establishing Okotoks. His ventures and adventures included freighting, oil, lumber and politics.

CROWSNEST PASS

From the final slopes of Crowsnest Mountain, Seven Sisters extends north like a great wing.

Crowsnest Pass area does not lie within any National or Provincial Park, and is not the tourist destination that Waterton is. Neither does it boast well-developed trail systems that Parks typically offer, but this is no detriment to scramblers. Geographically, the Pass is located north of Waterton Park near the eastern edge of the mountains but close to the provincial border. Travelling west of Pincher Creek, picturesque Highway 3 passes through a succession of towns, including Bellevue, Blairmore and Coleman, through the Pass and on into

British Columbia. The stretch is perhaps best known for the Frank Slide. In 1903, 74 million tonnes of rock broke off from Turtle Mountain, burying the coal mining town of Frank and killing some 70 residents. An interpretive centre located amid the debris just off the highway recounts the catastrophe.

Like Waterton, this region is subject to strong winds and falls very much under the Chinook's influence, resulting in a similarly drier and longer scrambling season. The quality of rock — limestone — is somewhat better than around Waterton though. Since many caves exist in the Flatheads, it is likely that as much spelunking as scrambling takes place at certain times of the year. Keep in mind that there is no rescue service. In case of an accident, searchers, if any, would be volunteers from neighbouring communities along with the RCMP, rather than Park Wardens doing a part of their job. No system of registration is available either.

Access The Municipality is serviced by Highway 3 running west from Pincher Creek and connecting through to Fernie and Elko in British Columbia.

Facilities and Accommodation Unlike Waterton, tourism is not the mainstay of Crowsnest Pass and life goes on much the same year-round. Nonetheless, there are several campgrounds in the area, as well as a few motels, service stations, grocery stores and restaurants. Limited camping and hiking supplies can be found in one of the local sports or hardware stores.

Information The Tourist Information Booth lies across from the hamlet of Sentinel, 6.6 km east of the B.C./Alberta boundary. It is closed during winter months.

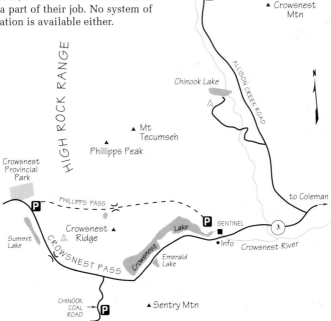

27

MOUNT TECUMSEH 2547 m

Difficulty Moderate scrambling on scree and slabs via south slopes
Ascent time 3-6 hours; 2-4 hours from Phillipps Pass
Height Gain 1175 m in total; 975 m from Phillipps Pass
Map 82 G/10 Crowsnest

Mount Tecumseh offers little in the way of difficulty or exposure and constitutes a pleasant outing in the Crowsnest Pass area. Either a four-wheel drive vehicle or a mountain bike is invaluable for the approach.

The actual ascent begins from Phillipps Pass which runs parallel to Crowsnest Pass 2 km to the north and separates Mount Tecumseh from Crowsnest Ridge, the latter crowned by a highly-visible microwave tower. The gravel access road through Phillipps Pass can be reached from either the east or west end as follows:

From the west, drive to Crowsnest Provincial Park, 2 km west of the B.C./Alberta Boundary on Highway 3. If you have a four-wheel drive vehicle or mountain bike, continue through the paved parking area, around a U-turn and head east along the cutline to cross a Texas gate. Make a brief detour left into trees rather than follow the road directly beneath the powerline, thereby reaching the open flats of the Pass. Park 4.2 km from Crowsnest Provincial Park, or 0.7 km east of a fenced-in, metal-clad building where the mouth of the drainage emerges at point 698017 near a steel hydro-line support tower.

From the east, drive into Sentinel on the north side of Highway 3 across from the Tourist Information Booth, 6.6 km east of the B.C./Alberta Boundary, and follow 26th Street 0.5 km past two right-angle bends and across railway tracks. Although cabled off, a gravel road connecting to Phillipps Pass begins on the north side of the tracks in front of a house on the hill. Hike or bike 3.3 km to the starting point identified above.

From the mouth of the drainage, hike upstream along the often-dry streambed draining the south side of the objective. No trail exists but travel is easy. Over time, abrasive action of water has carved solid limestone into a delightful series of "sinks" joined by twisting, smooth-walled channels which provide amusement as you try to ascend them directly. Alternatively, either side of the watercourse suffices to forego this idle fascination. Within an hour the streambed disappears and you reach a landscape of immense boulders, apparently wedged loose from steep slabs up to the right. Shortly beyond these crumbling mounds, turn sharply left to head on a more westerly bearing past a stand of evergreens into a confined scree basin flanked by the walls of Phillipps Peak and Mount Tecumseh.

Although you may be tempted to continue directly ahead for the top rather than heading left here, cliffbands of down-sloping rock complicate more direct lines to the summit. The suggested route allows you to sneak up from the south-west, mostly over scree and talus. Tramp either straight up or angle slightly right as you ascend from the basin, the objective being to gain the ridge above which leads easily to the summit lying east. Contrary to expectations, the crest of the ridge provides no airy maneuvers and is mostly a plod. A metal survey pole denotes the summit should there be any doubt.

Mt. Tecumseh and Phillipps Peak. Route starts from Phillipps Pass.   P Phillipps Peak,   T Tecumseh.

From the top, the most notable features of the landscape are Crowsnest Mountain and the Seven Sisters sitting impassively to the east of the High Rock Range. At one time, they were just one section of a massive and continuous thick sheet of limestone which was pushed in from the west, riding up over existing younger rocks beneath. The north-south line identifying this geological event is known as the Lewis Thrust. Crowsnest Mountain, one of the more visible reminders of this cataclysmic upheaval, has, through the erosive actions of Allison Creek, become a klippe — an outlier isolated from the main range.

One wonders why the high point located two pinnacles to the west deserves a separate title. Apparently, both Phillipps Peak and Tecumseh were in common use at one time until Tecumseh was officially adopted. As runner-up, the pinnacle to the west was later designated Phillipps Peak, although it hardly qualifies as a separate summit. An as-cent of Phillipps Peak beginning further west along Phillipps Pass and circling left to the west ridge would be a less technical as well as a less exposed route than the narrower south-east ridge between the two peaks.

More than one explanation exists as to the name of this peak and pass. Perhaps the most plausible theory suggests that Michel Phillipps of Elko, B.C. was the first white man to make use of this pass, apparently while scouting trapping territory in 1873. Bison had used it for centuries; Indians had for some reason avoided it. A now-defunct coal-mining town a few kilometres west also bears his name.

Tecumseh, a Shawnee Indian War Chief, rallied other Indian tribes into an allied force to combat American territorial expansion. His forces joined with those of the British and Canadian in 1812, a crucial time during the conflict. In a tragic twist of fate, he died fighting his own people.

SENTRY MOUNTAIN 2410 m

Difficulty Moderate scrambling via west ridge; minimal exposure
Ascent time 2-4 hours
Height Gain 1025 m
Map 82 G/10 Crowsnest

Diminutive Sentry Mountain stands guard over the windy gap of Crowsnest Pass where blustery west winds periodically whip the waters of Crowsnest Lake into a maelstrom of whitecaps. An ascent of the peak is an interesting and mainly non-technical ridge walk boasting fine views. Try from late May on.

The west ridge can be approached directly from almost anywhere within the first couple of kilometres of Chinook Coal Road. Since the initial and perhaps only real challenge is the actual crossing of Crowsnest Creek, in times of high water it is worthwhile scouting the least problematic crossing point. Late summer flows are typically only calf-deep but rocks are slimy.

Drive to Chinook Coal Road located 3.7 km east of the B.C./Alberta Boundary and 4.8 km west of the Tourist Information Booth on Highway 3 in Crowsnest Pass. Follow the road south for about 1.7 km and park alongside an open pit mine at the foot of Sentry Mountain's west ridge.

Cross the stream and tramp to the top of the limestone quarry. The terrain above is easy going through open forest as you hike steadily upwards. Occasionally a game trail materializes to coax you along, only to disappear at successive clearings. The ridge is broad for the initial few hundred metres of elevation gain, but becomes more clearly defined higher up. Whitebark pine contrast with bleached, twisted trunks stretching dry limbs skyward — a stark reminder of the enduring effects of a past forest fire. Underfoot, the rocky landscape is graced by patches of Kinnikinnik, also known

as Bearberry. Kinnikinnik is an Indian word which translates roughly to "smokeable". Rough it is, too. Not without reason were gifts of tobacco popular.

Enjoy the fine views to the south and west as you draw nearer to a bumpy part of the ridge. Now it becomes more interesting. With only about 275 vertical metres left to go, each hump seems to rise a little more steeply than the previous, suggesting a drop-off on the other side. This doesn't happen though. Erosion has seen to that. One brief notch requires a minor detour to the left on scree and ledges, but not until close to the top does a more serious-looking obstacle rear up. The entire ridge appears protected by a slabby, triangular rock face, seemingly straddling the ascent route. Tackling it directly is a challenge many won't bother with despite good solid rock. However, you can dodge around it on either side. A detour to the right necessitates a short scramble down to scree, followed by a plod back up and around this stony outcrop. The left side may be a better choice. It involves no elevation loss and with a bit of imagination you can almost see a path.

With this 20 or 30 m behind you, the actual summit is close. The ridge crest narrows dramatically in a couple of places, but except for one particular point where you must descend a 2 m step along the crest, the majority of airy moves are avoided entirely on scree along the right (south) side. For those unaffected by exposure, the most sporting line keeps directly to the crest.

The summit allows plenty of room for photography, eating and just plain old relaxing. One could probably wander south along the ridge for quite some distance before encountering any problems, although this would necessitate about 200 m elevation loss. Conversely, it would be equally easy to simply stare at larger peaks off to the west and debate which one might be 3359 m Mount Harrison. This was the last peak in the Rockies over 3353 m (11,000') to be "discovered" by cartographers working on new editions of maps about 1963.

It is evident from the photo that a multitude of ways exist to the top of Sentry Mountain, although many involve significantly more loose rubble than this option.

The west ridge of Sentry Mountain. Other route possibilities exist.

CROWSNEST MOUNTAIN 2785 m

Difficulty Moderate scrambling
via north side
Ascent time 2-4 hours
Height Gain 1100 m
Map 82 G/15 Crowsnest

"Like the sacred Fuji Yama of Japan, Crow's Nest mountain rises abruptly out of the earth, with no other mountains within miles", wrote P.D. McTavish in his account of the second recorded ascent of the peak in 1905. His relatively inexperienced party engaged in a circuitous route which seems to have encountered fairly serious climbing — entirely unnecessary using today's tourist route which, incidentally, was first ascended in 1915 as a solo venture. Locals ascend the peak with some degree of regularity and if you're in the area, it's a pleasant little jaunt. Try from June on.

9.6 km east of the Alberta-BC boundary and 14 km west of Frank Slide Interpretive Centre on Highway 3, turn north onto the Allison Creek Road. Follow the road for 9.7 km to a hiking trail sign. Park 0.3 km beyond on the cutline right-of-way.

From the parking area under the powerline, walk south 150 m to the marked path. The trail is well-used and easy to follow as it ascends to tree-line. Pine forest gives way to scree slopes at the north end of the peak where multi-pinnacled Seven Sisters Mountain abuts against the summit mass. Faded pink flagging exists periodically, but if you can't find it ascend scree to the right of the black waterfall marking the first band of cliffs. Climb through lower rock steps, then traverse left on a scree ledge below the black, wet walls of the second cliff. More than one trail can be found below the traverse ledge, but they should all rejoin at that point.

The second cliffband is breached by a long cleft to your left (east). Towards the top of this gully, move left, thereby avoiding entirely the damper, dirtier right branch. A ring piton is in place on the right side should anyone be carrying a rope and feel the urge to use it, but if the rock is dry it is unnecessary. Annoying dogs, children or partners could probably be tethered here too. Above this gully the way becomes evident, and no problems should be encountered as you zigzag up gentle scree for the remainder of the climb.

Gould Dome and more prominent Tornado Mountain dominate the view to the north, while Mount Ptolemy is the highest point in the cluster of summits lying nearby to the south.

Two theories confuse the origins of the Crowsnest name. One concerns a slaughter of Crow Indians by Blackfoot Indians near the town of Frank where they were corralled or in a "nest", but according to Reverend John McDougall, "on this trail through the mountains there was a nest which was occupied annually by crows" and it is this explanation which seems to be the more favoured of the two.

Descend by the same route.

Crowsnest Mtn. showing route of ascent. L lower rock steps, T traverse, G gully.
Photo: Tony Daffern

Photos: Gillean Daffern

Crowsnest Mountain: Above scree and first rockband the route traverses left below second rockband and enters gully on left to reach easy terrain above.

Entering the gully in the second rockband Note black streaks on wall.

CANMORE AND KANANASKIS

Mount Yamnuska	2240 m	easy	p. 40
Heart Mountain	2135 m	easy	p. 42
Mount Fable	2702 m	moderate	p. 44
Grotto Mountain	2706 m	moderate	p. 46
Middle Sister	2769 m	easy	p. 48
Mount Lady MacDonald	2605 m	difficult	p. 50
Mount Fullerton	2728 m	moderate	p. 52
Mount Glasgow	2935 m	moderate	p. 54
Mount Baldy	2192 m	difficult	p. 56
Mount Kidd S peak	2895 m	easy	p. 57
Mount Kidd	2958 m	moderate	p. 58
Mount Bogart	3144 m	moderate	p. 60
Mount Lawson	2795 m	moderate	p. 62
Mount Indefatigable	2670 m	easy	p. 64
Mount Hood	2903 m	moderate	p. 67
Storm Mountain	3092 m	moderate	p. 69
Mount Rae	3218 m	moderate	p. 70
Mount Arethusa	2912 m	difficult	p. 72
Mist Mountain	3140 m	moderate	p. 74
Mount Tyrwhitt	2874 m	moderate	p. 76

The three areas covered in this chapter, though not contiguous, fall within the eastern section of the Rockies known as the Front Ranges. The areas are Little Elbow Recreation Area, Kananaskis Valley through to Highwood Pass and Canmore corridor.

The topography of the three zones is similar. Mountain-building has created long limestone ridges, aligned north-west to south-east, with a noticeable "dip" or downward tilt to the south-west. In some areas, particularly in the Opal and Misty Ranges, compression during a period called the Laramide Orogeny thrust the strata into an almost vertical position. As shales and soft layers within the rock "sandwich" erode more quickly than others, a peculiar result occurs. West and south-facing ridges, which appear to provide plausible ascent routes, become cleft by notches and interrupted by pinnacles.

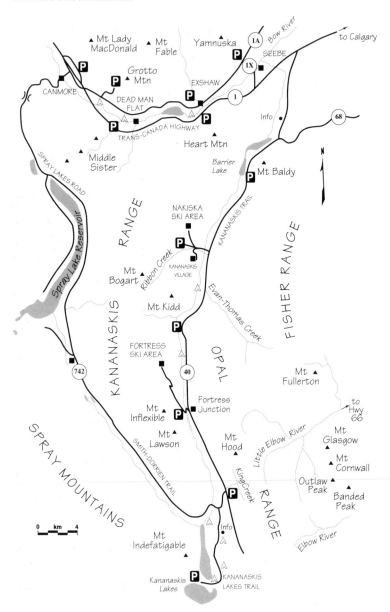

These pinnacles can be impressively steep on their westerly aspect and over-hanging on the east side. The softer the layer, the deeper the notch. Similarly, the narrower the ridge, the greater the problems. On this steeply tilted terrain, it is usually preferable to detour around these obstacles rather than take a head-on approach. On less steeply-bedded mountains, however, the south-west aspect generally provides the simplest way to the top. Although there are excep-tions, east faces in the Front Ranges are usually steep and technical in nature — certainly not scrambling terrain!

The Front Ranges are dry compared to more westerly areas of the Rockies. Un-derbrush is practically non-existent. This is *Chinook* country too — warm, westerly winds which bring about dras-tic and welcome rises in temperature during long cold winter months. As a result, these peaks have a long scram-bling season. When Lake Louise is rainy, Kananaskis may be just fine. In dry win-ters Lady MacDonald, Grotto and Heart Mountain are ascended year round. The most exciting season may be spring when furious Chinook gusts threaten to blow the unwary right off the top. This is especially fun for lightweight people! These same three peaks host sizeable populations of sheep which, in turn, host sizeable populations of ticks. Be sure to check thoroughly for the pests afterwards. I have found up to six on a single outing, even as early as March.

Some peaks in this chapter are within the boundaries of Peter Lougheed Pro-vincial Park, and except for those peaks north of the Canmore Corridor, are in-side the recreational area known as *Kananaskis Country*. While this is a favoured playground for many Calgar-ians and visitors, most folks do not ven-ture far above tree-line.

Routes are usually in condition by June. Peaks near Highwood Pass typically take a little longer. Despite occasional short-lived summer snow-squalls, these Front Range summits often stay in shape until late October or November. This includes Mount Rae, the loftiest at 3218 m. Most Front Range peaks are significantly lower than this, with the majority quali-fying for the "under 3000 metre" class.

Access To reach Little Elbow Recre-ation Area, drive to the village of Bragg Creek, south-west of Calgary, and follow Elbow Falls Trail (Highway 66) west. This road is closed beyond Elbow Falls from Dec 1 to mid-May. Kananaskis Val-ley is accessed by Kananaskis Trail (Highway 40) from the Trans-Canada 65 km west of Calgary. It continues south over Highwood Pass, then swings east and reaches Longview in the foothills and, eventually, Highway 2. Highwood Pass is closed Dec 1 to June 15 from Peter Lougheed Provincial Park turnoff to Highwood Junction. Smith-Dorrien/ Spray Road connects to Highway 40, 52 km south of the Trans-Canada, and pro-vides alternate access to and from Can-more (gravel road). Bow Valley Trail (Highway 1-A), running from Seebe to Canmore on the north side of the corri-dor, is used to reach Mounts Yamnuska, Grotto, and Fable.

Facilities The most complete range of visitor services is found in Canmore, including bars, grocery stores, gas sta-tions, laundromats and lodging. At Exshaw, on 1-A Highway, there is also a service station, small store and restau-rant — ideal for a dose of junk food after doing Mount Fable! Just east of Highway 40 turn-off is Chief Chiniki restaurant (service station and store also), while farther west at Dead Man Flat, the Husky

Gary Fauland begins the crux on Mt. Lady MacDonald.

stays open all night for those near-epics. If you're headed to Little Elbow Recreation Area, Bragg creek has restaurants, grocery stores, an ice-cream shop and a gas station.

In Kananaskis, limited groceries are available at Kananaskis Village Centre near Nakiska Ski area, otherwise the village is mainly hotels and bars. Mount Kidd RV Park has a small store. Farther south, Fortress Junction gas station offers a fairly good selection of food. Boulton Trading Post near Kananaskis Lakes has a cafe and store.

Accommodation The available accommodation covers the whole realm from campsites to pricey hotels. Throughout Kananaskis Country there are many campgrounds, but don't be surprised if most are full by late afternoon. A large campground can be found at Little Elbow Recreation Area if you're planning on spending time around there. Mount Kidd RV park on Kananaskis Trail is probably the most decadent of the lot. Until the snack bar and hot tubs close for the night though, you're not really roughing it. Public showers are available too. Campsites and less pricey motels can be found at Dead Man Flat. Ribbon Creek Youth Hostel offers overnight stays, as does the Alpine Club of Canada Clubhouse, about 2 km east of Canmore on 1-A Highway. Right in Canmore, friendly Haus Alpenrose, a Bavarian style chalet, provides bed and breakfast, dormitory-style or private rooms as well as cooking facilities. Climbing instruction, licensed guiding services and equipment rentals are also offered.

Information For general information, Tourism Alberta can be found at the west end of the gas station strip near Canmore west overpass. Kananaskis Country info is across from the Rose and Crown pub in Canmore's Provincial Building. Additional information centres include Barrier Lake on Highway 40; Kananaskis Visitor Centre in Peter Lougheed Provincial Park, and Elbow Valley on Elbow Falls Trail (Highway 66). There is one other info centre just off the Trans-Canada Highway by Bow Valley Provincial Park (on Highway 1-X) near Seebe.

Park Rangers are stationed at Elbow Ranger Station and Boundary Ranger Station at Ribbon Creek which is also the Emergency Services Centre. RCMP are stationed at Canmore and at the Ribbon Creek Emergency Services Centre.

TRAVERSE OF YAMNUSKA 2240 m
(Mt. John Laurie)

Difficulty from west, easy. From east, difficult downclimbing for 5 m
Ascent time 3-6 hours
for complete traverse
Height gain 900 m
Map 82 O/3 Canmore
(shown as Mt. Laurie)

Yamnuska is a popular early season outing and usually a beehive of activity. Easy access and quantity of routes attract scores of eager rock-climbers, particularly when bigger peaks are snowbound. Scramblers will find the ascent a good conditioner. Its easterly location renders it far less susceptible to inclement weather which plagues the Main Ranges to the west. The Yamnuska environs are well known for their diversity of plant life and, in early season, purple crocuses of varying shades carpet the hillside as you hike up grassy south-facing slopes. The most interesting ascent is an east to west traverse, utilizing enormous scree slopes for a rapid descent. Try from May on.

Yamnuska was formed by a movement known to geologists as the McConnell Thrust in which Eldon limestone of the Cambrian period (south-east face), was pushed up onto much younger and softer sandstones (lower slopes). The usual younger-over-older sequence of stratification or "layering" was reversed. The result is a geologically disorganized mountain with the demarcation line clearly evident.

Muddling about on the crux of east ridge route.
Photo: Kris Thorsteinsson

From Seebe intersection (Highway 1-X) on Bow Valley Trail (Highway 1-A), drive east for 2 km, then turn left and follow the gravel road for 1 km to a parking area and gate below Yamnuska.

From the grassy parking area, walk up the road past the gate and reach the upper bench of the quarry in a few minutes. Watch for a beaten path at the edge of the trees which forks almost immediately. Here you have a choice.

The left fork heads straight towards the mountain, rising in strenuous zig-zags to the base of the cliffs. If you reach a small spring within five minutes you will know you're on the descent trail and it will be necessary to backtrack to the correct trail further east. Upon reaching the base of the cliffs, circle around to the north-east side. From this point on, both branches of the trail coincide.

Yamnuska's back side showing traverse. W west side, E east ridge, C crux.

The right-hand fork is well-trodden and less demanding. For a considerable time it sidles along through aspen forest paralleling the peak, then curves left and climbs gradually to the ridge crest, topping out slightly east of Yamnuska. From the ridge crest, hike towards the mountain and around to the north-east side. The path descends to avoid a crumbly buttress, then traverses below it before rising towards the ridge crest above. On talus, angle west along the trail towards a shallow gully leading to a notch in a rock wall on the skyline. This is the easiest place; harder options exist some distance upslope.

The going is straightforward until you reach a steep rock wall which must be downclimbed into a broad gully. This is the crux. Most people choose to descend a 5-m groove into the gully, thinking it probably the least troublesome and exposed option. This groove is just slightly downhill of the summit ridge. The next obstacle is a steep wall rising in front of you alongside a notch in the summit ridge. This is most easily circumvented by descending scree to the right, then climbing back up to the ridge. Continue

to follow the beaten path. There are no further problems as you make your way to the sizeable summit cairn. Intrepid Calgary climbers, fresh from the mighty Pamirs Range in Russia, toted back a geological souvenir and it now huddles inconspicuously somewhere in the pile of more familiar Rockies limestone. No hybridization of species is expected to take place.

On **descent**, a beaten path in fine talus gives way to a section of slabs followed by coarser rubble as it winds down the west side and around the west end. In early season, snow persists on this aspect when the rest of the peak has dried off. This predicament has surprised more than one rock-climber shod in smooth-soled rock shoes. Once you are below the face again, first class descent scree allows a bee-line to tree-line.

Yamnuska is a Stoney Indian word meaning "mountain with sheer cliffs", and is in common use today. The official name is Mount John Laurie after a long-time friend of the Stoney Tribe who was instrumental in their many bureaucratic struggles for land claims, education and treaty rights.

HEART MOUNTAIN 2135 m

Difficulty easy, with one moderate step via north-west ridge
Ascent time 1.5-3 hours
Height gain 875 m
Map 82 O/3 Canmore

Heart Mountain merits inclusion for three reasons. It is handy to Calgary, it can often be ascended year-round due to Chinooks which blast the route bare and there are at least two variations for descent.

At one time the parking lot for Heart Creek Trail sat right at the foot of the mountain by the highway. To climb this popular little peak you parked, tramped 10 m to the foot of the ridge and pursued the beaten path to the top. Since then, the parking lot has been moved further west. Despite a longer approach the excursion remains a favourite early season pilgrimage for many — a chance to reintroduce sluggish muscles to the rigors of steep hiking.

Park at the signed parking lot for Heart Creek trailhead on the south side of the Trans-Canada Highway at Lac Des Arcs Interchange, 75 km west of Calgary and 36 km east of Banff.

From the parking lot, hike the trail paralleling Trans-Canada highway and cross Heart Creek to the foot of the ridge. The way is obvious. Follow the path as it climbs rapidly up the right side of the "heart" shape. Slabs encountered on the ascent are a pleasant change from scree, more exposed spots being easily avoided by a detour into the trees. Two-thirds of the way up the ridge levels off and you must scramble up a steep 2 to 3 m-high wall to regain the route. (Don't bother to continue along below this wall in hopes of finding an easier place to surmount it — there isn't one, despite a misleading, well-worn track.)

The first summit is soon reached after more easy scrambling. Many people are content to loll about and go no further, but a higher second summit lies some 25 minutes beyond to the south-east (318550). From that viewpoint there are a couple of options for the return trip. For visitors to the second summit, a pleasant **circuit** can be made by heading north-east, following a grassy ridge. Descend slightly down a grassy slope and tramp across a saddle to attain a minor high point (322554). This open ridge then begins to arc slightly left, coaxing you along on a windswept north-westerly course which descends gradually to mature forest below. This route sees considerable use and is easy to follow to the powerline. Quaite Valley trail then directs you back to Heart Creek.

An **alternative descent** down the west side of the mountain starts at a point almost directly below the true summit. It is shown on the map as an intermittent drainage. Descend open slopes towards Heart Creek as they funnel down towards a short drop-off guarded by a rock-wall on the right. This drop-off is easily turned and a game trail can then be followed into upper Heart Creek Valley. Wander downstream to meet the multi-bridge interpretive path.

For those who have reached the second summit and wish to explore further, an interesting extension can be added which takes you along a ridge leading south-east to twin high points (325537) overlooking Barrier Lake. Start by following the ridge south-east as it descends gently, losing hard-won elevation in the process. The crux of this extension is a drop-off situated about half-way between Heart Mountain and the two unnamed points. It can't really be assessed until you reach it. There is no way to avoid this brief test-piece. It must be downclimbed. The descent involves little more than 5 m of careful maneuvering, but is indeed a change of terrain. Keep in mind that you will be returning the same way, though climbing back up this trying rock step is a world easier.

Millions of years ago (between 45 and 85 million to be roughly precise), during a mountain-building period that geologists identify as Late Cretaceous to Middle Eocene, tremendous compressional forces folded the upper strata of Heart Mountain into a plunging syncline. When viewed from across the valley near Exshaw the reason for the name becomes entirely clear.

Photo: Gillean Daffern

North-west ridge from Heart Creek showing first summit.

MOUNT FABLE 2702 m

Difficulty A moderate scramble by south slopes to west ridge.
Ascent time 4.5-7 hours
Height gain 1325 m
Map 82 O/3 Canmore
(unmarked 242642)

Mount Fable is an attractive peak tucked behind Grotto Mountain and although the summit does protrude slightly above adja-cent peaks, it is not entirely evident as you approach the Rockies from the east. However, as you look north from Heart Creek it rises majestically across the valley, oblivious to the Baymag plant smoke stack in the foreground. Because of its dry easterly location, Mount Fable boasts a longer season than many. It is a viable choice as early as late May some years, but is not a well-travelled outing.

From the hamlet of Exshaw on Bow Valley Trail (Highway 1-A), follow Windridge Road on the east side of Exshaw Creek for 0.8 km to Mt. Lorette Drive. Park at the bridge.

View from the Trans-Canada Highway of Mt. Fable rising above Exshaw Creek. Route ascends easy slopes to left of rocky ridge.

An unusual view of the west ridge of Mt. Fable. Route ascends scree to col then follows skyline ridge.

From the parking area, cross the bridge over Exshaw Creek and follow the service road and an elevated water pipeline for some 10 minutes to a concrete dam. Depending on where you are wandering for this first section, there may be a hazard of flying rock from ongoing blasting in the quarry. Sunday is an exception.

Wade or hop over the stream and scramble up around the dam on the easier right side. Above the dam follow the creek on a good trail to a major side valley on your left (265622). This valley trends north-west and drains the south slopes of Mount Fable. Allow at least 1 hour to here. Now branch off up this tributary, rounding the base of the objective up scree to a col west of the final ridge. The easy west ridge is followed up slabs and scree to complete the ascent and apart from one narrow bit near the top there are no difficulties.

Due to the strategic location of Mount Fable in the arid Front Ranges, bushwhacking poses no problem. However in a dry year lack of water might be more of a nuisance, especially later in summer.

The first party to try this peak in 1947 returned frustrated, telling tales of having spent the day muddling around in the bush. Soon after, an entirely different group went at it and experienced no problems. They felt the defeated party's reasons for failure suggested an appropriate name, and, though not formally adopted, the title has gained local recognizance.

GROTTO MOUNTAIN 2706 m

Difficulty An easy scramble by either route.
Ascent time 2.5-5 hours
Height gain 1350 m
Map 82 O/3 Canmore

Grotto Mountain is a Canmore landmark that is ascended regularly, and some people begin the season with a visit as early as April. The approach walk is negligible, and several viable routes lead to the summit. Perhaps most popular are the two described here, which can be combined to allow a partial traverse.

Drive to Indian Flats Road 4.2 km east of Canmore on Bow Valley Trail (Highway 1-A). Continue past Bow Valley Riding Association's stable to the Alpine Club of Canada clubhouse. Limited parking may be available at the Alpine Club of Canada parking lot.

circumvents the majority of problematic sections. Beaten trails carefully winding around these obstacles suggest that although they are accomplished climbers, even Bighorn sheep prefer the easiest terrain, and when it exists, they typically make use of it.

Direct route

The shortest and most heavily-used route of any takes a direct line from base to summit, following quite close to the right edge of a massive gully draining the south-west slopes. From the parking lot by the ACC clubhouse, walk back down the road some 75 m and cut off to your left into the trees along the base of the hillside. Head towards the peak by going behind the fenced horse stable operation — mind the barbed wire. Cross a stream bed which flows in early season and hike up the hill on the other side, crossing pasture and grassy terraced slopes. Make your way towards open flanks to the right of the massive gully on Grotto's south-west side at 192600. There is no definite trail but travel is easy.

Keep to the left as you ascend. Occasional slabs scattered throughout forest provide a change of regimen, but since some of these slabs are both high and steep, you may want to simplify matters by staying very near the huge gully. This

North-west Variation

An **alternate ascent or descent route** lies more towards the north-west end of the mountain. This option is also in common use. It ascends the south-west flanks lying between Cougar Creek (unmarked on some maps) at the peak's north-west end and the huge gully at 192600 described above. From the ACC clubhouse, walk straight uphill towards the left end of the peak. Angle across pasture, through forest and ascend open grassy slopes towards the left skyline ridge. Follow alongside this ridge. The route is mostly straightforward but requires two short detours to overcome brief cliffbands. Turn the first cliffband via its extreme left (north) end and a short 3 m chimney. The second band gradually peters out as you traverse right (south).

After more forest, scree-line is reached. A long plod over yet more rubble past a false summit leads to the cairn and register. If you walk along the crest of the ridge, you may not even notice the tunnel through the rock beneath, mere minutes before the true summit.

The unnamed top at the north-east end of Grotto at 220620 presents demanding scrambling for anyone with more energy than restraint. Attack from the left side after descending scree to the intervening col, keeping in mind you must also re-ascend this tedious, unstable heap.

In 1858 James Hector and botanist Eugene Bourgeau of the Palliser Expedition scrambled some 300 m up a peak behind their camp. Their pursuits led to the discovery of a large high-roofed cave or grotto. Although there is an extensive cave system towards the south end of Grotto Mountain that has recently been sealed off to the public, this does not fit the description of Hector and Bourgeau's cave. We can only speculate where their exploits took them.

Photo: Gillean Daffern

Heading along the north-west ridge of Grotto, summit in background. Direct route ascends right skyline.

Grotto Mtn. showing direct route D, NW north-west variation.

MIDDLE SISTER 2769 m

Difficulty An easy scramble from Stewart Creek
Ascent time 2.5-5 hours
Height gain 1400 m
Map 82 0/3 Canmore

Like an in-between child, Middle Sister receives the least attention. Big Sister is highest, and garners the attention of scramblers; Little Sister is a technical rock climb on which climbers prove their mettle. Middle Sister just sits there, overlooked. Those who break with tradition have found the approach to the centre peak of Canmore's famous triad more laborious than the actual ascent. Also known as Second Sister, this summit possesses what is probably the most unique summit register anywhere in the Rockies. The distinctive container was supplied courtesy of Mr. M.B. Morrow, one-time president of now-defunct Canmore Mines who made the first ascent in 1921. Many years this peak is in condition by late May, but you may want to take an ice-axe for lingering snow patches.

The most direct way to Middle Sister is via Stewart Creek. As of Fall 1991, Three Sisters Resorts access road runs along the bench from Canmore to Stewart Creek but is closed to the public. It may be open by summer '92, in which case you will be able to drive to Stewart Creek. This access road starts 1 km along Spray Lakes Road in Canmore. If it is closed, the simplest approach will be from the shoulder of the Trans-Canada Highway near the "Visit Canmore" sign, just west of Dead Man Flat.

From opposite the "Visit Canmore" sign, hike west under the powerline right-of-way a short distance, then follow old roads through the intervening forest to gain Three Sisters Resorts access road and nearby Stewart Creek.

As of Fall 1991 there is a major road near Stewart Creek, close to a small canyon where the stream emerges from the valley. Cross the creek to the west side and gain an ancient exploration and mining road leading upstream. Along the way, you pass remnants of an old trestle. Shortly beyond, the road crosses over to the east bank and stays there apart from a short section up the middle of the creek. Without warning it ends on a steep sidehill immediately east of Little Sister. Almost nothing of the upper valley can be seen from this point.

Follow the creek and soon the stream forks. Take the right branch. Some 10 minutes later a major avalanche gully coming down from Little Sister meets the main drainage. Continue straight ahead. The terrain is rocky; steep hillsides confine you to the drainage making you wish for an easier way where none

Photo: Kris Thorsteinsson

Register on Middle Sister.

Stewart Creek and Middle Sister from Wind Ridge showing ascent route. B Big Sister

exists. Impatience has sent some climbers dashing for the summit as soon as a col becomes visible on the right. Their enthusiasm has been dampened quickly by the realization that they are headed for the wrong col — the one between Little Sister and the objective. Avoid this inclination and persevere ahead.

The streambed curves and climbs a little more steeply to escape tree-line. Since the simplest line to the Big/Middle Sister col is a rising traverse from left to right, the further up-valley you wander, the more obvious the route becomes. You will be below and east of Big Sister at the point where you begin angling up. It seems like a long plod to

reach this spot and it is, but fortunately you have gained a good percentage of the total elevation by now. Upon tramping up slabs and scree to the Big/Middle Sister col the effort is justified. Views throughout the length of Canmore corridor are revealed.

No difficulties exist for the remaining walk to the summit. Although close, it is clear there is no easy way up nearby Big Sister from this vicinity. The normal ascent route lies on the south side and is approached from Spray Lakes Reservoir. After you have signed the book and admired the panorama, return the same way.

49

MOUNT LADY MACDONALD 2605 m

Difficulty Final 50 m of normal route difficult and exposed scrambling; Alternate route moderate
Ascent time 2.5-4 hours
Height gain 1300 m
Map 82 O/3 Canmore (unmarked 179649)

Mount Lady MacDonald offers a pleasing early-season conditioner with an exciting finish. Blessed with low snowfall, it is possibly the most-frequented scramble in the Canmore vicinity, although not everyone reaches the true summit. The crux that deters some parties can be circumvented. Try from April on.

From Elk Run Industrial Park on the east side of the Trans-Canada Highway at Canmore, drive (or walk) 0.5 km up rough road by Cougar Creek to a rock dam. Park here.

Although innumerable possibilities exist, the most popular trail begins just before a boulder dam built at a narrow neck of the Cougar Creek canyon. Incidentally, in the wet spring of 1990, record rains swelled this trickle to an angry torrent and obliterated the breakwater entirely, causing anxious moments for home owners in the subdivision downstream. Several found they had suddenly acquired riverfront property.

On the open hillside to the left, immediately before the dam, pursue an obvious path ascending briskly up the grassy slope. Other trails converge within minutes, resulting in a well-travelled track. Make sure you branch right at a fork after about 10 minutes; the left trail is a meandering horse path. Again the route climbs steeply through woods and grassy glades, passing a peculiar patch of fine, greenish shale. Openings provide increasingly better views over the valley.

Numerous sheep haunt these slopes, each graciously providing ample fodder for wood ticks. Unfortunately, some ticks prefer humans, and find us easy targets as we loll on open slopes in the sun, leading them on with our exhaled carbon dioxide. Springtime is the worst — or the best, if you're a tick. Keep this in mind as you relax in one of the many clearings near tree-line.

The trail is easy to follow as it parallels a sparsely-wooded ridge en route to a small plateau below rubble slopes. Notice the metal launch ramp for hang gliders.

The most common and sporting finish ascends diagonally above the hang-glider launch. There is a semblance of trail as you trudge up scree, then angle left across more scree towards the highest visible point. Although this is not the true summit, it is very near and the way soon becomes obvious. The terrain changes quickly to a narrow ridge which leads to the cairn a few minutes to the north-west. The final connecting ridge is startlingly precipitous on the east side; steep and slabby on the west side. Of the 50 or so metres of this final arête, some 15 m are the most demanding. You may find yourself crossing at least some part au cheval — straddling it. Alternatively, you can also attack from below, climbing a 20 m high groove in slabs, though most find the ridge to be the lesser of two evils.

For anyone hoping to attain the summit but unenthusiastic about the prospects mentioned above — sporting or not — they need not be disappointed. There is an alternative. From near the hang-glider ramp, stay low down on the scree slopes and traverse well around towards the north-west, missing entirely both the exposed connecting ridge and the groove. Once you have circled around, scramble up and gain the ridge top beyond the narrow bit. This option would also be the easier route of descent.

From the summit, ski-tourers in particular should recognize Robertson Glacier and Mount Sir Douglas set between Mount Lougheed and Big Sister. To the north-west, Mounts Temple and Hungabee of the Lake Louise group are apparent.

The peak is named in honour of Lady Susan Agnes MacDonald, wife of Canada's first Prime Minister. The First Lady certainly displayed an adventurous spirit on her premiere visit to the Rockies. Enthralled by the scenery, she heightened her experience further by riding outdoors, perched precariously above clattering rails on the locomotives' cowcatcher. Despite strong objections by Sir John, who thought the idea ridiculous, she audaciously rode from Lake Louise through Kicking Horse Canyon towards Golden, British Columbia, declaring her vantage point "quite lovely".

Lady MacDonald from Cougar Creek. S summit, P plateau, A alternative route.

MOUNT FULLERTON 2728 m

Difficulty A moderate scramble via north-east slopes and ridge. South-east ridge difficult
Ascent time 3-5 hours
Height gain 1050 m
Map 82 J/15 Bragg Creek

Mount Fullerton is one of the Front Range peaks which comes into condition comparatively early on in the season. This makes it a good May starter. Depending on whether or not you enjoy testing your route-finding skills, there is a choice of options. For variety, both routes can be incorporated in a traverse.

Photo: Gillean Daffern

Looking west to Mt. Fullerton from the forks of Nihahi Creek. N NE ridge, S SE ridge.

Park at Little Elbow recreation area west of Bragg Creek on Highway 66. Unless you are a registered camper, the normal parking area is to the left before the campground entrance.

North-east Ridge

Walk west through Elbow campground to Little Elbow trailhead. This was once a driveable road and is well-suited to mountain bikes for the initial 3.5 km to Nihahi Creek. Allow 20-30 minutes on foot to reach this point. A signed trail to the right leads you into a broad, alluvial streambed — typically bone-dry — running north between Nihahi Ridge on the right and Mount Fullerton on the left.

After approximately 1-1.5 hours from Little Elbow trail, the main branch of the valley turns abruptly westward and circles around to the north side of

the objective. At this point you can either follow the small, rocky drainage which emanates from an amphitheatre at 445320 on the north-east side of Mount Fullerton and gain open slopes on the right, or you can cut directly through trees towards this same open north-east ridge. The way up then becomes obvious. Only near the top, where a few short rock steps arise, does this route amount to anything more a walk, and before you know it, you're on the summit. A lower, unnamed point to the west is a 20 minute walk away.

If you choose to ascend by the more challenging south-east ridge, this north-east ridge route makes for a no-nonsense descent. However, the stony plod back along Nihahi Creek can hardly be called inspiring.

South-east ridge

The long south-east ridge is a much more challenging undertaking. You can gain it at Little Elbow trail just west of Nihahi Creek, or, to escape the first two hours of forest, proceed up Nihahi Creek as described above. Ascend open slopes and dry drainages at any of several places on the east side of Fullerton. This will lead up to the south-east ridge proper. Continue north, passing two lesser but well-cairned summits along the way, to where real route-finding begins.

Contrary to more typical Front Range topography where strata are bedded with a noticeable dip to the west or south-west, the rock layers here dip to the east. This geological anomaly presents a challenge. Beyond the second cairned high point the ridge narrows and ends abruptly in a 5-10 m drop. As you look further ahead, successively lower strata rise up ramp-like only to drop-off, apparently in a similar manner. The test then is to find a practical descent route down to successively lower ledge systems as you progress westward. Some of these shelves are easier to descend on the left (south) side; at least one is downclimbed on the north side. Snow lingers on the north side and adds to the difficulty, so save this route until June at the earliest.

It is not necessary nor advisable to traverse along the narrow "neck" which appears to connect to the main summit mass. Instead, you should actually be a couple of ledge systems below and on the left side of this. A few small cairns appear promising. Once you can turn a particularly large skyline buttress on its left side you have virtually surmounted all obstacles. Circle around this point to a more south-westerly aspect and so to the summit. Return via the easier north-east ridge.

C. P. Fullerton, for whom the mountain was named, was at one time Chairman of the Canadian National Railways.

Heading down the north-east ridge.

MOUNT GLASGOW 2935 m

Difficulty A moderate scramble via snow or scree slopes and west ridge
Ascent time 4-6 hours
Height gain 1310 m
Map 82 J/15 Bragg Creek

An ascent of Mount Glasgow offers a close look at a notable tetrad of mountains which includes nearby Mount Cornwall, an unofficially-named summit called Outlaw Peak and lastly, Banded Peak which rounds out the foursome at the south end. The most identifiable feature of the group may be the east slope of Mount Cornwall.

This stony incline holds snow like moss holds moisture. By mid-summer it usually retains some of the only snow on the horizon. Of the two summits to the south, Banded Peak's triangular shape is characterized by a conspicuous horizontal rockband just below the top which further contributes to the group's unique appearance. With mountain bikes and proper logistical planning, the general cluster can be conquered in a long day — but more about that later. The route is frequently in shape by mid-June.

Park at Little Elbow recreation area west of Bragg Creek on Highway 66. Unless you are a registered camper, normal parking is to the left of the campground entrance.

All the rubble you can stand. The NW side of Mt. Glasgow showing route from Little Elbow trail.

The 1.5-2 hour approach on foot can only be described as drudgery. Therefore, it is suggested you cycle this flat section of old road. From the parking area follow the road through Little Elbow campground past the gate and continue along Little Elbow trail. Once you cross the blue

Photo: Kris Thorsteinsson

Extending the trek. A bizarre figure approaches the summit of Outlaw Peak. Mt. Cornwall behind

bridge to the south side of the river, watch for the first drainage that intercepts the trail at 443271. Depending on time of year, this small stream may or may not be flowing and you could miss it entirely. Emanating from a stony valley between Glasgow and an 8900' outlier (460258) to the north, the streambed provides access to easy west-facing slopes leading to Glasgow's barren summit.

Follow along the left side of the drainage, keeping above the first section where it becomes a narrow canyon. Once this chasm peters out you can boulder-hop straight up the creekbed. Upon reaching the far (south-east) end of the valley, turn right and outflank steep walls via a long scree slope (snow-covered up to June or later) which then directs you around onto the rubbly west ridge and the summit. No problems exist, but this route is perhaps one of the strongest arguments of any for using ski-poles on scree.

Ambitious types will note the apparent simplicity of **extending the trek** south to the gentle ridge of Mount Cornwall. Cornwall is easily traversed south-east to Outlaw Peak (455205), also easily negotiated, and finally to Banded Peak which completes the lengthy march. None of these peaks presents any difficulties. A straightforward exit lies down the east fork of a south-east trending drainage (462195) between Banded and Outlaw Peaks and leads to Big Elbow trail at 478178. You intercept the trail two drainages before the bridge carries the trail to the south bank. This rambling traverse has been accomplished by parties approaching opposing ends of the circuit on mountain bikes, then swapping for the return pedal back to Little Elbow recreation area. Allow one long day.

Glasgow and Cornwall were cruisers which played a prominent role in the 1914 Battle of the Falkland Islands.

MOUNT BALDY 2192 m

Difficulty One difficult step via south-west shoulder; exposure
Ascent time 1.5-3 hours
Height gain 700 m
Map 82 O/3 Canmore
(unmarked 369528)

Mount Baldy is close to Calgary, close to the road and close to the ground. Of late it has been mistakenly called Barrier Mountain ever since publication of a climbers guide to the cliffs at the base known as "Barrier Bluffs". To add further confusion, a low hump near Evan-Thomas Creek to the south is called "Old Baldy". During World War II, when the nearby Forest Experiment Station was an internment camp, prisoners were occasionally allowed to make ascents of the mountain — if they promised to return. Nowadays the precipitous lower cliffs often swarm with rock-climbers escaping a different kind of internment. Often possible as early as April.

Park on the shoulder of Kananaskis Trail (Highway 40) 13 km south of the Trans-Canada Highway and 1.6 km past Barrier picnic area turn-off at the south end of Barrier Lake.

From the starting point past Barrier Picnic area, ascend through thinning trees and slabby outcrops to the ridge. The drop alongside increases as you progress. About two-thirds of the way up a rock step necessitates a brief but exposed down-climb of 4 m — good practice for more demanding climbs! Shortly beyond, a slabby gendarme guarding the way must be overcome, starting at a short crack. It looks more challenging than it actually is. After this bit of maneuvering, the remaining trek to the summit cairn consists of easier scree and slabs presenting few difficulties.

Unfortunately there is no simpler descent route, but the crux step is easier on return as you will be climbing up.

Route ascends south-west shoulder. G gendarme.

Photo: Kris Thorsteinsson

MOUNT KIDD SOUTH PEAK 2895 m

Difficulty Easy to moderate scramble
via south-west side
Ascent time 3-5 hours
Height gain 1290 m
Map 82 J/14 Spray Lakes Reservoir

The south peak of Mount Kidd is easily
ascended from Galatea Creek and,
though slightly lower than the north peak,
constitutes an agreeable outing. There
are little in the way of problems.

South peak viewed from a point above Guinn's Pass.

Drive to Galatea Creek parking lot on
Kananaskis Trail (Highway 40), 32.9 km
south of the Trans-Canada Highway.

From the Galatea Creek parking lot, follow the trail towards Lillian Lake. After
about one hour of steady walking, just
before the trail crosses over the stream to
the south bank, head straight off to the
right through a short belt of willows.
Clamber up the steep grassy hillside towards a broad avalanche gully (247365).
The going is straightforward.

Wander through stunted poplars
which somehow manage to survive
yearly avalanches, and in short order
reach low-angle slabs. These allow rapid
elevation gain. A couple of brief but
steep rockbands near the summit ridge

are easily skirted to the left, whereupon
coarse but not tedious rubble delivers
you to the actual ridge crest. A few
notches thwart progress on the crest
proper; trudge and scramble alongside
these on the right (south) side. The summit lies only minutes away.

Though longer and rather illogical,
an **alternate route** is also viable from
Guinn's Pass should you be in that area.
Head east, traversing below the ridge
crest on the south side until beyond the
first high point (237374). If you stick to
the actual ridge crest, an unexpected
drop-off will require considerable elevation loss and bothersome backtracking to circumvent it on the south side.
Beyond that detour, no further obstacles exist.

MOUNT KIDD 2958 m

Difficulty A moderate snow/slab/scree
ascent via south-east bowl
Ascent time 3-6 hours
Height gain 1350 m
Map 82 J/14 Spray Lakes Reservoir

Although the approach is minimal, Mount
Kidd is a steep, unrelenting grind best
done about late May or June when maxi-
mum glissading is possible. Knowledge of
ice-axe self-arrest is imperative during
these months. Your safety also depends
on accurate assessment of snowcover
clinging to the steep walls above the bowl.

Because much of the route is visible from
the highway, most parties prefer to wait for
evidence of a major or climax avalanche
having occurred before heading up. That
way, a lot of the snow will be compacted
into the lower third of the bowl.

Anyone who is unsure of their judgement would do well to postpone their attempt until later in the season when the
climb involves only scree and slabs. This
route is ascended with a certain degree of
regularity by various parties, many of
whom time their ascent to coincide with the
terrific glissade descent that is possible.

Drive to Galatea Creek parking
lot on Kananaskis Trail (Highway 40), 32.9 km south of the
Trans-Canada Highway.

From Galatea parking lot follow
the hiking path to Lillian Lake
across the Kananaskis River and
Galatea Creek to a T-junction.
Take the right-hand option —
Terrace trail. Follow the trail as
it parallels Kananaskis River on
the east side of Mount Kidd,
reaching a streambed in 20 minutes. In spring this icy cold
brook is an ideal place to chill
victory drinks for the trip back.

Leave Terrace trail and follow
vestiges of path along the right
edge of the stony, often-dry streambed towards the huge bowl
draining the peak's east side.
Scramble up the right-hand side
on firm rock ledges in the company of waterfalls and soon you
are into the wide bowl. This
bowl is a classic example of a

Heading for the huge bowl on Mt. Kidd.
Note avalanche debris.

58

Upper part of bowl route up Mt. Kidd as seen from Kidd's south peak.

geological feature known as a syncline, which in this case indicates the northern terminus of an ancient upheaval called the Lewis Thrust. On the upper half of the route the left-most gully is least problematic. The next gully to the right is similarly easy once you're actually in it, though you must traverse steeper slabs to reach it. A line of pinnacles separates these two routes. Though slabs and scree present few obstacles en route to the summit, the sustained angle will tire you. Take your ice-axe if there is snow on this slope. If new snow has fallen within a few days before your attempt, you should go elsewhere.

There are sections of this route where rock steps lie beneath the snow. Water flowing over these steps can weaken the overlying snow, and there exists a very real hazard of falling into an icy, wet chasm between the rock and ice. Use caution as you go. Similar circum-stances on Mount Niblock in June 1989 resulted in a fatality.

Although the incline is better suited to staring groundward, you may notice a peculiar window near the base of a high buttress along the skyline ridge connecting north and south peaks. Although the south peak is also attainable (described on page 57) the complex nature of this intervening ridge prevents any thoughts of traversing the two summits.

Upon topping out of the ascent gully, you are greeted by a view of Mount Bogart just across Ribbon Creek. A gentle ten minute walk along a stately ridge leads east to the true summit. In early season, be wary of the massive cornice that often lingers a few metres beyond this point.

John and Stuart Kidd once ran a general store and trading post at the nearby settlement of Morley; the mountain was named for the latter.

MOUNT BOGART 3144 m

Difficulty Moderate by south slopes from Ribbon Creek
Ascent time 4-6 hours
Height gain 1650 m
Map 82 J/14 Spray Lakes Reservoir (shown incorrectly on edition 2, should be 1 km SW at 235412)

Mount Bogart, the second highest point in the Kananaskis Range, is one of the more easily-identified peaks as you approach the Rockies from Calgary. The prominent triangular summit often retains snow when surrounding mountains appear bone-dry. Though vistas are far-ranging, sections of the lengthy excursion are rather long and uninspiring. Challenges are limited and moderate in nature. Try from late June on.

Drive 23.4 km south of the Trans-Canada Highway along Kananaskis Trail (Highway 40). Turn west and follow signs to Ribbon Creek parking lot.

From Ribbon Creek parking lot, follow the popular Ribbon Creek hiking trail beginning on the north side of this swift stream. This is a well-trodden trail but for this ascent you will probably be starting early enough to beat the onslaught. Continue along the wide pathway for 11 km to Ribbon Creek Falls. Beyond the campground the trail angles up from the base of the falls and switchbacks to cross a rock slide.

Leave the hiking trail once you reach the stream emanating from a high valley at the south end of Mount Bogart (235395). This watercourse may not always be flowing. Follow goat trails up green slopes on the left-hand side of the drainage until it becomes simpler to cross over. A brief stint of scrambling along ledges and up a gully leads through the rockband to an unexpectedly large, meadowy cirque complete with various alpine flowers and a tiny pond.

This basin offers a perfect opportunity to relax and contemplate the remainder of the outing. The much-foreshortened perspective of the route makes the summit appear deceivingly close. Don't be fooled. After a couple of hours of slogging up treadmill-type scree to reach the final uplift, it will have become painfully obvious just how deceptive the earlier picture really was. Upon reaching the rockband guarding the top, a prominent but fairly narrow gully cleaves this hurdle. This is the crux. Persevere, the end is in sight. Once you surmount this feature the rubble relinquishes, allowing you to stumble to the cairn at last.

The summit vista is a rewarding one. On a clear day, visibility extends over 100 km to the Purcell Range of British Columbia. A short jaunt along the ridge grants a birds-eye view of the three Memorial Lakes one airy kilometre below you, the ultimate source of Ribbon Creek's north fork.

Mount Bogart is named for geologist Donaldson Bogart Dowling who explored the area for the Geological Survey of Canada in 1904.

Whew! What a walk! The normal route on Mt. Bogart begins above Ribbon Falls. The only challenge is a rockband near the top. R Ribbon Creek, B basin, C crux.

MOUNT LAWSON 2795 m

Difficulty A moderate scramble via east-facing scree slopes
Ascent time 2.5-4 hours
Height gain 1200 m
Map 82 J/14 Spray Lakes Reservoir

Mounts Lawson and Inflexible parallel Highway 40, together forming a continuous eight kilometre long escarpment of the Kananaskis Range. In spite of its proximity to a major road, Mount Lawson is seldom ascended. Perhaps the kilometre of dense pine forest lying between the road and the foot of the mountain dis-

suades enthusiasts. This is too bad. Early season ascents may offer a good glissade on the return, and ambitious types can extend the venture to include Mount Inflexible (3000 m) as well.

As viewed from Fortress Junction, a deep basin carved in the escarpment separates Mount Lawson from slightly higher Mount Inflexible to the north. A smaller, triangular dish-shaped area lying left of this deep basin funnels into the approach drainage. This drainage grants a direct line of access to Lawson's summit.

Access is via Fortress Ski Area access road, 41.8 km south of Trans-Canada Highway on Kananaskis Trail (Highway 40). Park at the first switchback beyond the bridge.

From the first switchback where you park, the initial test is to get into the correct drainage. It will be the second one you come to after departing Fortress Ski Area access road. Taking a compass bearing on its approximate location before blundering off blindly into dense forest makes sense. The first drainage, the larger of the two, flows well down into the trees. Cross this to the second drainage; smaller, overgrown and dry until you advance well upstream. It will require some 25 minutes to reach this drainage from your car. As you progress up the streambed a couple of waterfalls encountered can be scrambled around easily along the right-hand side. Shortly after, brief larch-treed slopes are reached. By this point you are granted virtually uninterrupted views the length of the Kananaskis Valley below a backdrop of steeply-tilted summits in the Opal Range.

Keep to the left of the aforementioned dish-shaped area on easy-angled, rocky terrain. From the road this section appears much steeper than it actually is. Toil up oodles of debris occasionally punctuated by short bluffs of broken, angular limestone typical of Front Range peaks. Soon a hasty walk brings you to the wide summit area. The highest point sits slightly south of where you top out.

Looking west, a narrow, hidden valley tucked between parallel ridges of Mounts Lawson and Kent is revealed. Much further south and west the dominant forms of Mounts Joffre, King George and Assiniboine preside over lower peaks.

As is now apparent, determined souls can readily traverse north along the straightforward connecting ridge to reach neighbouring Mount Inflexible (3000 m).

Should you decide to add this to your agenda, the least problematic way down is to retrace your steps to Mount Lawson and descend the ascent route. It is possible to descend scree and downsloping slabs on the west side of Mount Inflexible to James Walker Creek, but

Don't let the trees deter you!
Route begins from Fortress ski area access road.

even with two cars at your disposal this trek would be of questionable merit.

On the return, if you have your ice-axe, there may be an opportunity to glissade, should you (and the slope) be so inclined. In one heavy-snowfall year, a mid-June outing granted a glorious, long sitting glissade of more than 300 m — a quick and cheeky way of losing height and body heat.

Major W.E. Lawson was a topographer with the Geological Survey of Canada; Inflexible was a battle cruiser engaged in the Battle of Jutland. Kent was a newspaper reporter.

MOUNT INDEFATIGABLE 2670 m

Difficulty From Mount Indefatigable hiking trail to south peak: easy.
To north (true) summit and traverse to south peak: moderate scrambling with brief exposure
Ascent time 2-4 hours to south peak only; 4-6 hours for entire north to south traverse.
Height gain 1000 m
Map 82 J/11 Kananaskis Lakes

Scenically located, this strangely-named peak lends itself well to a traverse in either direction. North to south is slightly easier. Right from the beginning the views are expansive as you rise along an airy precipice overlooking Upper and Lower Kananaskis Lakes. Doing even one of the two summits is well worth the effort. Try from late June on.

Park at North Interlakes parking lot at the far end of Kananaskis Lakes Trail.

South Summit

From North Interlakes parking lot, walk along the lake shore trail and cross the dam. Follow the Mount Indefatigable hiking trail which branches right almost immediately past the dam. After initially passing through shady coniferous forest, this popular path soon gains the open escarpment along the east side of the mountain. To ascend the south peak, watch for a well-used trail diverging left about one hour along, just before a sign indicating the hiking path continues directly ahead. This is perhaps 10 minutes before the end of the hiking trail proper — also indicated by a sign. Follow this side trail as it climbs steadily making a no-nonsense line up grass and talus for the south summit and a repeater tower straight above.

A significant number of people typically make this trek on a sunny day, the lure of a summit drawing them away from the comfortable grade of the heavily-used hiking trail.

The normal route to Mt. Indefatigable north (highest) summit. Note figures on top.

North Summit & Traverse

To reach the north peak, continue to the end of the Mount Indefatigable hiking trail. Once you pry yourself loose from the wooden bench that has been positioned for breath-taking views of the Opal Range, scout around for a well-used spur trail. This ever-improving trail enters larch forest and in 25 minutes emerges unexpectedly at a beautiful alpine tarn high on the east side of the peak (co-ordinates 303123).

Continue to wander up grassy, flowered meadows to the east ridge which leads directly to the north peak — the true summit. This route is becoming increasingly popular. Over a four year period a plainly visible path has been beaten into the dirt and rubble for much of the way, and the register book is filling rapidly.

Heading for gully below the north summit.

Opposite: The typical view of Mt. Indefatigable from Interlakes parking lot. S south summit.

Magnificent Kananaskis Lakes from the south summit.

The ridge between the 2 summits.
North summit is just right of centre

As you ascend, keep just left of the ridge, scrambling up a broad gully for the final 50 m. This is the crux. Though not steep, the rock is notably loose for this final bit and dislodges easily. You should refrain from following directly below anyone else. The day I made this ascent I was blissfully unaware of a localized thunderstorm brewing out of sight in the west. Without warning, lightning struck the cairn a mere 50 m above, causing me to beat a temporary but hasty retreat. From the summit, the panorama is superb.

The head-on perspective of the exposed ridge connecting to the south peak suggests it may have its moments. A good part of the distance, however, is merely hiking. The rock is firm when most required and a few of the exposed sections can be skirted by descending slightly to scree on the west side. Unavoidable exposed stretches are brief. Allow 30 minutes to reach the south peak. When done marvelling at the

Royal Group, glaciated Mount Joffre and the Opal Range walk south for about 200 m past the tower to an obvious path descending the east side. This steers you back to the Mount Indefatigable hiking trail below.

MOUNT HOOD 2903 m

Difficulty Moderate scrambling via west slopes and south ridge
Ascent time 3.5-6 hours
Height gain 1300 m
Map 82 J/11 Kananaskis Lakes

Mount Hood is one of the less conspicuous peaks in Kananaskis' Opal Range. Despite the lack of technical difficulty it is not a high-traffic mountain. The somewhat bushy approach discourages the casual wanderer, and because it is not evident from the road it does not attract a lot of interest. This is one of the few viable scrambles in the Opal Range. In general, the topography of the group does not lend itself well to unroped climbing. Try from late June on.

Drive to King Creek, 52.5 km south of the Trans-Canada Highway on Kananaskis Trail (Highway 40).

The approach to Mount Hood can be as involved as the actual climb itself. Though you can reach the peak via Hood Creek further north, it is preferable and less problematic to approach from King Creek despite additional distance.

Follow the interpretative trail through King Creek Canyon. When the stream forks, follow the left branch which leads north below steep, grassy avalanche-prone hillsides — the realm of Bighorn Sheep and the occasional grizzly. Continue up valley to the headwaters. This allows you to attain the broad saddle between Mount Hood and the long unnamed ridge to the west. From the saddle, straightforward gully scrambling takes you to the col between Mounts Hood and Brock. Both the rubble and the steeply-dipping, shattered rock encountered on the south ridge up to the summit are indicative of most south ridges found throughout the Opal Range. A geological movement called the Lewis Thrust is chiefly responsible for the pronounced tilt of peaks in this range and, since the same selected layers comprise each peak, climbing is remarkably similar throughout the area.

Sir H.L.A. Hood was rear admiral and commander of the ship Invincible which was sunk at The Battle of Jutland.

Ascent route showing G gully, C col and south ridge to summit.

Photo: Gillean Daffern

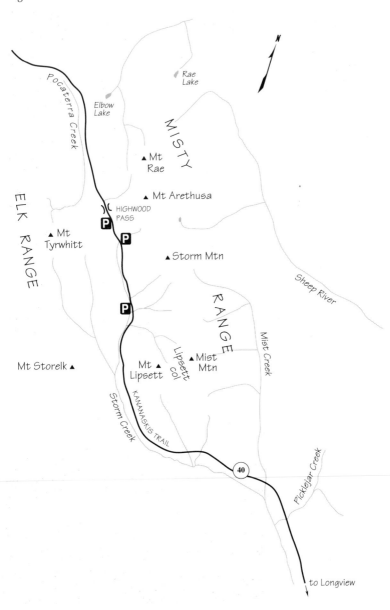

N

Pocaterra Creek

Rae Lake

Elbow Lake

M I S T Y

▲ Mt Rae

▲ Mt Arethusa

HIGHWOOD PASS

P

P

ELK RANGE

▲ Mt Tyrwhitt

▲ Storm Mtn

Sheep River

P

R A N G E

Mist Creek

Mt Storelk ▲

Mt ▲ Lipsett

Lipsett col

▲ Mist Mtn

Storm Creek

KANANASKIS TRAIL

40

Picklejar Creek

to Longview

STORM MOUNTAIN 3092 m

Difficulty A moderate scramble via south-west slopes
Ascent time 2-4 hours
Height gain 1050 m
Map 82 J/10 Mount Rae

Storm Mountain is a worthwhile outing with a brief and easy approach through larch meadows. A high starting point in the dry eastern Front Ranges guarantees a minimal amount of effort will be wasted plodding through forest to attain the summit. Try from July on.

Park at Lost Lemon Mine information sign, 4.4 km south of Highwood (Pass) Meadows parking lot on Kananaskis Trail (Highway 40). Note: Road closed Dec 1 to June 15.

Either one of two valleys can be used to reach the peak. The narrower valley 0.5 km north (at 455045) of the parking area is where the descent route emerges, so it may be a more logical starting point. The idea is to gain the end of the 500 m-long south-east ridge of Storm Mountain (co-ordinates 461052) via easy south and west-facing talus slopes, and follow it north to the true summit. If you begin from the more southerly (460042) valley by the Lost Lemon Mine information sign, start ascending the scree slope on your left at the last bit of meadow.

From the high point at the south end of the final ridge at 461052, a convenient, wide ledge 5 m below the narrow crest on the east side is followed until slightly beyond the low point. Then you scramble back

up to the crest and so to the top. From the summit there are fine views west of Mount King George (3422 m), monarch of the Royal Group, while Mount Sir Douglas (3406 m) rises skyward to the north-west.

For a rapid **descent** use the west ridge. A tricky but short connecting ridge leads to loads of scree and slabs which deliver you to the main valley with little fuss, effectively slashing the return time to as little as one hour.

Geologist Dr. George Dawson, a to-pographical surveyor and Director of the Geological Survey of Canada named the peak for storm clouds observed on the summit.

Two possible approaches to Storm Mtn from Hwy 40. S Storm Mtn, D descent route.

Photo: Gillean Daffern

MOUNT RAE 3218 m

Difficulty A moderate scramble via south slopes and south ridge
Ascent time 3-5 hours
Height gain 1000 m
Map 82 J/10 Mount Rae

As seen from the road, Mount Rae is not a peak of great beauty. Nonetheless, at 3218 m, it is one of the highest peaks in either the Front Ranges or the Kananaskis region. This fact, along with the ease of approach, guarantees it will remain a popular ascent despite the amount of scree involved. Try this trip from July on.

Drive to Highwood Meadows parking lot at Highwood Pass on Kananaskis Trail (Highway 40). Note: Road closed Dec 1 to June 15.

Ptarmigan Cirque hiking trail leads quickly past alpine meadows to the normal route. At the rear of the cirque veer left on the path and churn your way up a wide scree gully to a col between Mount Rae and unnamed 9900' (428089). The left side of this chute is less tiring. As you top out, views to the north burst forth, making the col an ideal location to snack and ponder the upcoming section. A minuscule glacier directly below you is the ultimate source of Elbow River and Calgary's drinking water — mind where you relieve yourself. In early snowfall years this secluded, shrinking bulge of ice becomes popular with eager telemarkers. Its sheltered aspect holds snow well.

From Ptarmigan Cirque, route ascends broad gully to col then follows ridge to summit. P pinnacle. C cirque

Photo: Clive Cordery

Nearing the top of Mt. Rae via the south ridge.

As you continue along the ridge, small gendarmes — pinnacles along the ridge — can be easily skirted until a threateningly large one, which looks like the summit, straddles the entire ridge. If there is snow on the north-facing slopes to the left of this pinnacle, it is possible to circle right to surmount it by climbing a small slab into a chimney beneath a monstrous chockstone. In dry conditions this is unnecessary. The logical way is to detour left onto scree and ledges high above the glacier and regain the ridge further along. Further on, the next gendarme on the ridge crest forces some awkward moves. Most hurdles you are confronted with, including the narrow summit ridge, are avoided by keeping left.

James Hector, surgeon and geologist of The Palliser Expedition named Mount Rae for fellow surgeon John Rae. Rae was, among other postings, doctor on a Hudson's Bay Company ship and participant in the search for the lost Franklin Expedition.

MOUNT ARETHUSA 2912 m

Difficulty Difficult scrambling via south
slopes and south-east ridge
Ascent time 1.5-3 hours
Height gain 750 m
Map 82 J/10 Mount Rae

Mount Arethusa is a short but exciting
scramble in the scenic Highwood Pass
environs. The ridge-like shape of this
peak does not suggest any great degree
of challenge. However, the normal ascent

route up the mountain is fairly exposed in
several places and dictates a rating of
"difficult" in contrast to the "moderate"
grading given neighbouring Storm Mountain and Mount Rae. Like adjacent peaks
though, the higher than usual starting
elevation ensures an easy approach. The
optional descent route, with its few brief
challenges, cuts the return time by half.
Try from July on.

Park 1.3 km south of Highwood (Pass)
Meadows parking lot on Kananaskis
Trail (Highway 40). Note: Road closed
Dec 1 to June 15.

From the parking spot, follow the left-
hand side of the drainage through open
forest. Wasting no time, this quick approach soon leads to alpine meadows
in the upper valley with Arethusa's
summit directly north. Towards the

south end of the peak are several spots
where the horizontal band of cliffs
guarding the mountain has eroded
away, allowing you to attain the crest of
the south-east ridge without problem.
Having done so, continue north along
this interesting crest, making short diversions as required until you reach a
point where you must descend a step in
the ridge. This point is the crux.

Photo: Kris Thorsteinsson

*Ascent route gains ridge at right-hand end near low point in the ridge, then follows close to the crest.
Summit lies at left-hand end.*

Photo: Gillean Daffern

Close-up view of Mt. Arethusa. C crux, D descent.

Carefully scramble down an exposed 5 m chimney on the east side, then immediately switch to the easier left (west) side, thereby bypassing the narrow, rotten crest of the ridge ahead. Once past this section, no further difficulties are encountered. From the road, the crux section appears as an obvious notch followed by a procession of small pinnacles.

If all snow has melted, the west ridge yields a quick **descent route** and is much simpler than retracing the ascent route. From the summit, traverse ledges and short slabs diagonally for about 50 m to a deep notch. This notch is visible from the highway. A curving gully leads steeply back to your left (south) to open meadows and the road. Note that snowy or wet conditions would render this descent gully appreciably more demanding. Tattered rappel slings in one steeper spot gives credence to this assertion.

Arethusa, a woodland nymph in Greek mythology, was changed into a stream to escape her pursuers. In yet another surprising but more recent transformation, she became a British Light Cruiser, and was sunk by a mine in 1916.

MIST MOUNTAIN 3140 m

Difficulty Moderate by north-west ridge; difficult from Mount Lipsett col
Ascent time 4-7 hours
Height gain 1050 m
Map 82 J/10 Mount Rae
(Mt. Lipsett unmarked at 470013)

Although eclipsed by nearby Mount Rae, Mist Mountain is one of the loftier viewpoints in Kananaskis. Located close to Highway 40 in the dry Highwood area, it readily lends itself to a traverse. The most direct route approaches from the north, utilizing broad gullies to gain the easy north-west ridge. Try this ascent from July on.

Park at Lost Lemon Mine information sign, 4.4 km south of Highwood (Pass) Meadows parking lot on Kananaskis Trail (Highway 40). Note: Road closed Dec 1 to June 15.

North-west Ridge Route

From the parking area, cross the road and follow a game trail along the left bank of the stream (451028) to minimize bush until open slopes are attained. It is not necessary to go very far up the creek;

the widest and perhaps easiest gully leading to the north-west ridge is also one of the first that you reach (462027). In fact, many adjacent gullies also offer potential scramble routes to the ridge above. You can study these at your leisure from the road. Upon reaching the north-west ridge, you have gained the majority of elevation. A dizzying escarpment to the east will probably convince you to tramp along the rubbly, but less vertiginous west side of the ridge to the summit rather than walk the actual crest.

Photo: Clive Cordery

Two routes on Mist Mountain allow a traverse. L Mt. Lipsett, M Mist Mountain, LC Lipsett col

Photo: Gillean Daffern

View from summit looking along NW ridge.

Lipsett Col Route

An ascent from the col between Mount Lipsett and Mist Mountain offers more challenge, particularly if you choose ridges and ribs instead of rubbly gullies.

To reach Lipsett col, follow the stream as for the north approach, continuing south-east to the headwaters. Scramble up whichever line suits your fancy and arrive at the col between Lipsett and Mist. From Lipsett col there are plenty of routes to gain the south ridge of Mist Mountain. Keep in mind that some rock ribs and pinnacles overhang on east-facing aspects and may require that you backtrack at times. Sections are surprisingly firm and afford delightful scrambling. Unfortunately, once you reach the south-east ridge of Mist Mountain, the quality deteriorates quickly. Exasperat-ingly loose scree, unpleasantly reminiscent of the final 200 m up Mount Engadine, concludes the ascent. Lacking a paddle, ski poles are the best alternative for such tiring terrain.

By combining these two routes a pleasurable high-level **traverse** can be completed which could also include minuscule Mount Lipsett (2482 m).

Mist Mountain was named by geologist Dr. George M. Dawson for, not surprisingly, mist on the mountain — mist that might have been caused by small hot springs lying just east of the peak. It is also entirely possible that he named it when naming neighbouring Storm Mountain, in which case the phenomenon would likely have been weather-related. Mount Lipsett is named after Major-General L.J. Lipsett, C.M.G., Canadian Expeditionary Force.

MOUNT TYRWHITT 2874 m

Difficulty A moderate scree/slab scramble via east ridge
Ascent time 3-5 hours. Allow 1-2 hours from Grizzly Pass.
Height gain 650 m
Map 82 J/11 Kananaskis Lakes

Mount Tyrwhitt offers an easy approach, an interesting scramble and the least elevation gain of any ascent described in this volume. In autumn, brilliantly coloured larches make the approach especially scenic, but it is not to be taken for granted — this alpine terrain is fragile and easily damaged. It takes years for plant life to recover from big boots. Whenever possible, try to use existing trails to minimize your impact.

When we ascended this mountain we were greeted by a sea of clouds filling Elk Valley to the west. Ensconced in a misty, flowing blanket of white, distant summits of the Joffre and Italian Groups barely penetrated this veil. One could only imagine how the complete scene would have looked. For those attempting this outing, try from July on.

Drive to Highwood Meadows parking lot at Highwood Pass on Kananaskis Trail (Highway 40). Note: Road closed Dec 1 to June 15.

The rock arch on the east ridge

From Highwood Meadows follow the interpretive trail through charming larch meadows. When this path heads right, leave it and follow along a seasonal drainage channel past a boulder whereupon good animal trails lead you over a ridge to a small pond. Continue on game trails and reach the stony environs of Tyrwhitt cirque, the headwaters of Pocaterra Creek's south-west fork. Keep to the left and angle towards Grizzly Col, the low saddle on the left (east) side of the objective. Tedious scree mocks your efforts until you gain the Pass — a feature unnamed on map 82 J/11 which separates Mount Tyrwhitt from an unnamed point immediately east. This saddle is an ideal place to catch your breath before undertaking the remaining 250 m to the top.

Grizzly Col sits squarely atop the Lewis Thrust, a geological event which pushed massive sheets of older Rundle limestone over younger and more easily eroded shales and sandstones. Running north-west to south-east, the fault line extends from Glacier Park in the United

Mt. Tyrwhitt from the north showing the east ridge in profile. G Grizzly col, A arch, R alternate return route

States north to Mount Kidd. This explains the rather abrupt change in terrain underfoot as you continue up. The transition takes you from shale and fine scree to higher-angled slabby rock.

As you clamber up the east ridge summit-bound, a unique 5 m high window through the mountain about half-way up suggests legitimate reasons to linger. The camera can be put to good advantage here. Sharp eyes may be able to pick out this window from the highway.

Rather than retrace the same route from Grizzly Col, there is an **alternate return route** which follows the ridge to the north-east. It is readily followed to a minor high point above the parking lot, then descended to your vehicle. Along this traverse are thin layers of coal sandwiched within a Cretaceous rock unit known to geologists as the Kootenay Formation. Dating back 100 to 140 million years ago, this period recalls the era of dinosaurs. These coal seams represent massive beds lying farther south in the coal belt of Crowsnest Pass, as well as in other locations in Kananaskis, including the reclaimed mine site on Mount Allan.

Admiral Sir R.Y. Tyrwhitt was leader of the British destroyer flotillas during World War I.

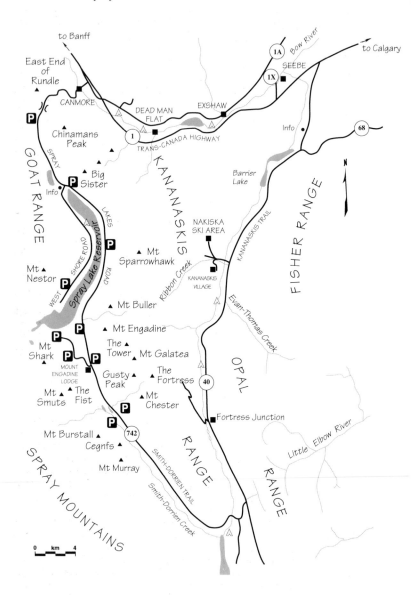

SMITH-DORRIEN/SPRAY AREA

East End of Rundle	2590 m	easy	p. 81
Chinamans Peak	2408 m	easy	p. 82
Big Sister	2936 m	moderate	p. 84
Mount Nestor	2975 m	moderate	p. 86
Mount Sparrowhawk	3121 m	easy	p. 88
Mount Shark	2786 m	moderate	p. 89
Mount Smuts	2938 m	difficult	p. 90
The Fist	2630 m	difficult	p. 92
Mount Murray	3023 m	moderate	p. 94
Mount Burstall	2760 m	difficult	p. 95
Mount Buller	2805 m	moderate	p. 96
Mount Engadine	2970 m	difficult	p. 98
The Tower	3117 m	moderate	p. 100
Mount Chester	3054 m	easy	p. 102
The Fortress	3000 m	easy	p. 104
Mount Galatea	3185 m	difficult	p. 106
Gusty Peak	3000 m	easy	p. 108

Spray Lakes Road and Smith-Dorrien Trail provide access to peaks in this chapter. Together they form a mainly gravel-surfaced road running some 65 km from Canmore, past Spray Lakes Reservoir to Highway 40 in Peter Lougheed Provincial Park.

Peaks along this corridor have much in common with those in the preceding chapter — all are *dip-slope* limestone summits in The Front Ranges. Precipitation is slightly higher than in areas to the east, so the scrambling season is reduced a bit. Some peaks on the Continental Divide may take until July to clear of snow. The nature of these ascents is similar in character to other scrambles in The Front Ranges. Rock is frequently down-sloping. While smooth slabs are sometimes encountered on easier routes, there is also a considerable quantity of shattered and angular rock which requires care due to looseness.

The alpine environs of Chester Lake is perhaps the most heavily-visited region and offers several ascents.

Access from Canmore is via Spray Lakes Road which begins after you cross Bow River bridge. You can also reach the south end of the corridor from Kananaskis Valley and Kananaskis Trail (Highway 40). Turn off Highway 40 at King Creek (50 km south of the Trans-Canada

Mt. Assiniboine dominates the scene from Mt. Shark. At right is ascent ridge.

Highway) and head along the Kananaskis Lakes Trail towards Kananaskis Lakes. Smith-Dorrien Trail branches right in 2.5 km. As a matter of interest, when coming from the east the distance to Chester Lake parking lot is nearly identical whether you drive to Canmore and then south on Spray Lakes Road or go down Highway 40, then north up Smith-Dorrien Trail. The former is a little quicker since more of it is paved.

Facilities and Accommodation At present, there is little development along the Smith-Dorrien/Spray corridor, but with K-Country's penchant for construction the picture may well change in future. So far, the only lodging available is at Mount Engadine Lodge. This privately-owned inn, 37 km south of Canmore, offers meals, accommodation and licensed guiding services. The only campsites are around Kananaskis Lakes in Peter Lougheed Provincial Park or across Three Sisters Dam on the west side of Spray Reservoir. The Spray campsites are unimproved and free, however, the Alberta Government is considering charging for sites.

There is a wide variety of accommodation and services available in Canmore, including a couple of pubs favoured by the outdoor crowd. For more detailed information, see the introduction to Kananaskis Country.

Information and Rangers For information on trails and conditions, Kananaskis Country maintains a small information centre (pay phone available) and Ranger Station at Spray Office just before Three Sisters Dam, 17 km south of Canmore.

EAST END OF RUNDLE 2590 m

Difficulty An easy scramble via south scree slopes
Ascent time 2-4 hours
Height gain 950 m
Map 82 O/3 Canmore
(unmarked 105598)

The East End of Rundle is a good early season objective that requires minimal

effort. This is not, of course, Rundle's true summit but the eastern extremity of the 12 km-long uplift. Steep faces above the canal host several rock-climbing routes; the gentle south slope serves as a climbers' descent route. It is also an increasingly popular early season jaunt for scramblers and hikers as the snow on the route often disappears by mid-May.

Follow Spray Lakes Road from Canmore townsite past the Canmore Nordic Centre to Whiteman's Pass and Goat Creek parking lot, 8.6 km past the Bow River bridge.

From the parking area, hike back along the road and look for a trail near the first set of powerline poles on a small bluff east of Goat Creek parking lot. Follow this path through ever-thinning forest to tree-line where scree slopes and a short cliffband lead to two minor summits, interesting vantage points which have, on at least one occasion hosted skimpily-clad — not to mention surprised — sun-worshippers. No guarantees though.

The Rundle traverse is often started from this end, and although the initial stages are largely hiking, sections towards the main summit become technical and require a rope.

East end of Rundle showing ascent route from Whiteman's Pass.

CHINAMANS PEAK 2408 m

Difficulty An easy ascent via south-west scree slopes
Ascent time 1-2 hours
Height gain 700 m
Map 82 O/3 Canmore (unmarked 123573)

Chinamans Peak is short, simple and steep. Both the ascent and the summit crest will make you gasp. The referenced co-ordinates indicate the actual location of

Chinamans Peak and it is this point that concerns rock-climbing enthusiasts and scramblers alike. Although a higher summit (2680 m) lies south-east, it is unnamed and considered a separate entity. Lately, Chinamans Peak has become a popular launch site for para-sailers. With minimal elevation gain and a season that starts comparatively early, this is a good outing to begin the season. Try from mid-May on.

Follow Spray Lakes Road from Canmore townsite past the Canmore Nordic Centre to Whiteman's Pass and Goat Creek parking lot, 8.6 km past the Bow River bridge.

Cross the road and walk uphill to the bridge over the canal. Immediately behind a small building, find a well-worn path beaten into thick moss. This is the climbers descent route and serves as a no-nonsense means of ascent to non-climbers or anyone appreciating good views with a minimum of effort.

The route climbs steeply through thinning coniferous forest, diverging into several trails higher up. After a total gain of some 500 m tree-line is reached (watch for flagging on return) and the western panorama begins to unfold. A final plod up 300 m of scree and slabs brings you to the summit above a giddy drop down the north-east side. Please don't be tempted to roll rocks down this precipice — there may be climbers on it! Mount Temple is the highest peak visible to the west; part of the impressive Royal Group can be observed to the

Photo: Gillean Daffern

As seen from East End of Rundle, the back side of Chinamans Peak is just a short, steep hike.

south and, should anyone care, smoggy Calgary huddles on flat lands to the east.

It is feasible to **traverse** over to the higher unnamed point at 127567, but there is a considerable amount of route-finding among ledges and gullies, making it much more difficult than what you've just accomplished. Should you opt to try, it is an easy walk-off from that summit to the canal via the west slopes. Otherwise, **descend** the same way.

Chinamans Peak was first ascended in 1886 by a Chinese miner, Ha Ling, employed by the now-defunct Canmore Coal Mines. He was reputed to have made the round trip in six hours — possibly via this same route — and by the following year the name was in common local use. Almost another hundred years were required for official recognizance, and it was still omitted on the next edition of the topo map.

Opposite: Looks like a race!
A busy day on the final scree slopes.

BIG SISTER 2936 m

Difficulty A moderate scramble via
south-west slopes
Ascent time 3-6 hours
Height gain 1200 m
Map 82 O/3 Canmore

Big Sister is the Grand Dame of the much-
photographed trio which graces the skyline east of Canmore. The standard route
is from the south-west side. From Spray

Lakes Road both the exact location of the
summit and the most feasible route are
puzzling to pinpoint as numerous parties
have discovered in the past. Many groups
end up retreating in the face of increasingly steep, overlapping slabs before even
getting within striking distance of the top.
The correct route is a pleasant outing and
is often possible from July on. Descend
via the same route.

Follow the Spray Lakes Road from Canmore. Park in the gravel pit across the
road from Spray Dam, 17.3 km beyond
the Bow River bridge in Canmore.

From the gravel pit notice the massive
gully system draining the south-west
side of the peak. The normal route begins on the slope immediately left of
the bottom of this gully. An unmistak-
able trail ascends diagonally through
forest keeping well above the left-most
branch of this gully system. From your
vehicle then, walk straight towards the
base of this gully and watch for the trail
on the hillside to the left. You should
have no trouble finding it.

Continue along this path as it rises
hurriedly through thinning forest. As
you near a short steep rockband — apparently barring further progress — two
options exist. The simpler choice is to
descend the short wall on your right
into the gully (you may have to backtrack to the key "groove"), or, alternatively, climb the rockband ahead by its
left-hand side. Travel is straightforward
again. Just before the summit, two
steep-walled pinnacles poised on the
ridge are skirted on the left. This brief
section could be treacherous and require an ice-axe if snowy.

The summit views throughout the
length of the corridor are agreeable, and
now you can peer down towards unas-
suming Little and Middle Sisters. Although the smaller of these two is a
technical rock climb, Middle Sister is an
easy scramble approached from Bow
Valley and Stewart Creek and is described elsewhere in this book. Unfortunately, the most glaring landscape feature may be the ugly mine scar on Grotto
Mountain, a result of quarrying limestone for use in cement.

First indicated as Three Sisters on
George Dawson's coal map of 1886, this
homologous cluster had previously
been called Three Nuns. Individual
peaks are locally known (unofficially) as
Faith, Hope and Charity.

Opposite: Big Sister from Spray Reservoir.
P pinnacles on summit ridge,
D short downclimb.

MOUNT NESTOR 2975 m

Difficulty A moderate scramble by south slopes; some exposure near top
Ascent time 2-4 hours
Height gain 1250 m
Map 82 J/14 Spray Lakes Reservoir

Besides boasting impressive views of Spray Lakes vicinity, it is virtually impossible to get lost on the way up Mount Nestor. While the east face of the peak flaunts a technical and much-frequented rock-climbing route, the south aspect provides the normal way off. This southerly route is also a pleasant, no fuss way to get up the peak since it begins right next to the road. Try from late June on.

From the bridge over the Bow River in Canmore, drive Spray Lakes Road for 17.3 km, then cross Three Sisters Dam to West Shore Access Road. Follow this winding gravel road for a further 13.4 km until the road makes a quick "S" turn as it rises up a small hill. Park near the top of this hill.

Walk east down the road to the bend at the base of the hill and notice a cairn or flagging beside the overgrown drainage. There is usually an animal trail visible here which follows along the right side just above thickets of willow and poplars choking the dry streambed. Within minutes it hastens through these poplars, crossing the drainage to follow up the left margin until, within some 20 or 30 minutes of starting, you escape the trees. Here you can appreciate unrestricted views back south towards Mounts Birdwood, Smuts and Sir Douglas.

Continue straight ahead past stunted krummholz and carpets of bearberry which soon give way to rubble. The route is self-evident. The trough you are traipsing up has been caused by a folding of strata which forced it into a U-shape, known to geologists as a syncline. The trough widens significantly at the top where you attain the crest of a rocky ridge separating this trough from

Photo: Kris Thorsteinsson

A closer view of upper south slopes

a much broader gully. Cross this broader gully and hike up onto a rounded shoulder on the skyline — the only logical place to go. The angle eases as you approach the summit ridge.

Near the top it becomes necessary to descend about 10 m and cross a brief connecting ridge to the true summit, which is all of 2 m higher. The first time I got to this point years ago one quick glance scared me off. Had I taken a closer look, overall lack of exposure and difficulty would have been apparent, and there would have been no need to return later. There are, however, a couple of moves just past this arête that some might consider mildly exposed.

The summit does not grant a lot of room for lounging about, but there is sufficient space to sit and admire the skyline. Many big peaks are conspicuous including Mount Sir Douglas, Mount Ball and the distant Goodsirs but as is so often the case, Mount Assiniboine steals the show.

On return, a pleasant variation is to **descend** the broad gully paralleling the one used for ascent. Near the bottom, it curves gently left and rejoins the route of ascent.

Ships involved in The Battle of Jutland have lent their names to the majority of peaks in the Kananaskis locale; this is but another on the list. Nestor was a destroyer which went down during the conflict.

Opposite: Mt. Nestor across Spray Lakes Reservoir. A variation can be taken on descent.

MOUNT SPARROWHAWK 3121 m

Difficulty Easy via west scree slopes
Ascent time 3.5-6 hours
Height gain 1350 m
Map 82 J/14 Spray Lakes Reservoir

Mount Sparrowhawk is a simple ascent overlooking Spray Lakes Reservoir. Little difficulty can be found on the open west slopes of this giant mound of rubble. At one time, ambitious plans were conceived to make Mount Sparrowhawk the site of downhill ski events for the 1988 Winter Olympics, but despite much opposition nearby Mount Allan was chosen. The sole reminder of this proposition now exists merely as a few discarded poles, snow-fencing and markers littering the upper portion of the proposed area. Plod up this peak from late June on.

Drive to Sparrowhawk picnic area on Spray Lakes Road, 26.3 km south of the Bow River bridge in Canmore.

Much of the south-west slopes are devoid of vegetation so you can walk up most anywhere to the small summit bump. We tramped up the right side of a drainage, and then left of the rock spur (207440), located west-south-west of the summit. Plenty of options are available. However, be aware that the highest point of the aforementioned rock spur ends in a drop-off, and does not connect to the summit mass.

As you approach the top, circle around the final summit cliffs via the right (south) side and hike up the east aspect to the top.

Mount Sparrowhawk is not named after a bird, as you might expect, but after a World War I battleship — which was probably named after the bird.

Clear sailing ahead! Upper part of Mt. Sparrowhawk showing rock spur to right. The route dodges to right at summit block.

Photo: Kris Thorsteinsson

MOUNT SHARK 2786 m

Difficulty A moderate scramble
by the north ridge
Ascent time 3-5 hours
Height gain 1000 m
Map 82 J/14 Spray Lakes Reservoir

In spite of its lower elevation, Mount Shark is a good vantage point that hosts few visitors. Technical difficulties are few, but lack of a recognizable path beyond Karst Spring probably dissuades the curious wanderers from exploring much farther. Try from July on.

Mt. Shark from the east side. The peak is normally ascended via the north (right skyline) ridge.

Drive to Mount Shark/Mount Engadine Lodge access road on Smith-Dorrien Trail/Spray Lakes Road, 6.4 km north of Burstall Pass parking lot and 38.2 km south of the Bow River bridge in Canmore. Follow this access road to its end at the Mount Shark parking area.

From the parking area hike or bike the wide trail 4 km to Watridge Lake. Continue on foot to boisterous Karst Spring below the north ridge of Mount Shark which provides the normal route of access. Head straight up the hillside. With a little persistence and the odd scratchings of an animal trail, determination will deliver you to less claustrophobic surroundings, leaving the cacophony and the crowds far below. This initial short but compulsory stint of bushwhacking may be the crux of the entire jaunt.

As you gain tree-line, scattered patches of spruce relinquish territory to Lyall's Larch, and soon you are scrambling unimpeded up angular, slabby limestone typical of the Front Ranges. On a calm day, the reservoir mirrors multi-peaked Mount Lougheed in shades of aquamarine.

Just when you think the going is good, the ridge narrows. This mountain is not to be won so easily after all. Frequent detours right avoid more exposed sections of the ridge crest, and after a couple of false summits punctuated with much rotten rock you finally stumble onto the crumbling summit. Lush, green valleys, sparkling lakes and icy, precipitous faces merge to surround you in a stunning rendition of mountain landscape.

On the **return**, simply retrace your ascent route. Heading towards noisy Karst Spring below may be least problematic. Flagging on trees does not indicate a preferred route in this instance.

89

MOUNT SMUTS 2938 m

Difficulty Difficult scrambling via the
slabby south ridge
Ascent time 3.5-6 hours
Height gain 1075 m
Map 82 J/14 Spray Lakes Reservoir

Mount Smuts presents demanding
scrambling on steep, slabby limestone
ribs. Sections of the route are also exposed — "exhilarating" comes to mind. It
is likely that some parties don the climbing
rope during the outing, though confident
scramblers will find it unnecessary if the
rock is dry. Try from July on.

Photo: Leon Kubbernus

Nearing the summit.

Drive to Mount Shark/Mount Engadine Lodge access road on Smith-Dorrien Trail/Spray Lakes Road, 6.4 km north of Burstall Pass parking lot and 38.2 km south of the Bow River bridge in Canmore. Follow the access road west for 0.9 km, crossing Smuts Creek en route, and make the first left turn onto an old logging road. Park in a few metres.

From the parking area, walk south along an old logging road. After some 20 minutes, just before the road drops down to Commonwealth Creek, bear right on another logging road, usually flagged, which leads towards the vociferous brook. A rough path on the north side continues into the valley.

Hike alongside meadows and beaver ponds towards Smuts Pass, the high saddle at the end of the valley between Mounts Smuts and Birdwood. Slightly before the pass, on the north side of the valley, ascend a large scree-cone fed by a scree gully. This gully is the result of the softest layer of a steeply-tilted rock sandwich steadily eroding away. Although you can't tell by the foreshortened view up this gully, the summit of Mount Smuts lies to the right. Trudge up this gully; it narrows higher up before the left wall finally peters out completely. Now you must ascend the slabby right-hand wall — choose your spot. From here on, near vertically tilted ribs of firm Palliser limestone undulate directly to the summit, alternating high-angle steps with stretches of plodding.

Once you begin the real scrambling there is not a lot of variation possible. Upon gaining the initial slabby right-hand wall above the gully, it becomes quickly apparent whether or not the game is to your liking. Remember, the descent follows the same route and is sure to be more intimidating looking down.

There are no pornographic overtones associated with the rather peculiar name; Jan Christiaan Smuts was an exemplary statesman and general of the Union of South Africa.

Opposite: The south ridge of Mt. Smuts — arguably the most difficult scramble in this book.

THE FIST 2630 m

Difficulty A difficult and exposed scramble by south slopes
Ascent time 3-5 hours
Height gain 770 m
Map 82 J/14 Spray Lakes Reservoir (unmarked 149301)

Shaped like a clenched fist thrusting skyward, this unofficially-named craggy little peak boasts an exciting finish. Al-though sitting only 5 km north-west of Mud Lake, it has entertained very few ascents. The imposing vertical rock walls presented on its most commonly seen sides impart an air of futility. The secret lies in attacking from the south flanks — hidden from the road — which offer markedly fewer challenges and a reasonable line of ascent. Try from late June on.

Drive to Mount Shark/Mount Enga-dine Lodge access road on Smith-Dor-rien Trail/Spray Lakes Road, 6.4 km north of Burstall Pass parking lot and 38.2 km south of the Bow River bridge in Canmore. Follow this road west for 0.9 km, crossing Smuts Creek en route, and take the first left turn onto an old logging road. Park here.

From the parking area a few metres off the Mount Shark access road, walk south along an old logging road. After some 20 minutes, just before the road drops to Commonwealth Creek, bear right on another logging road, usually flagged, which leads towards the vociferous brook. A rough path on the north side continues into the valley.

Pleasant hiking along the stream for about an hour leads to open, marshy meadows and wide avalanche slopes on the right. These slopes provide access to the connecting ridge between The Fist and its west-erly neighbour Mount Smuts. No doubt each party will form their own opinions regarding the best route up this slope. It being winter, I found skis to be superior. In summer, probably following up the small drain-age in the centre of the ava-lanche slope would be easiest and most direct. The ascent of

The Fist from Commonwealth Creek, showing route of ascent up avalanche slopes to the Smuts/Fist ridge.

This photo shows the Smuts/Fist connecting ridge and the ramp-like gully which cleaves the summit block from left to right.

this hillside represents the majority of the total elevation gain for the ascent.

Once you top out on the Smuts/Fist connecting ridge, traverse along the south side of the objective without losing any height, aiming for a narrow ramp-like gully. The summit sits slightly north (left) of what would be a natural continuation of the aforementioned Smuts connecting ridge. Any high points either straight ahead (north-east) or slightly to the right of this steepish gully are merely lower "knuckles" of The Fist.

The ramp-like gully tops out on a brief, airy ridge leading north. At this point you are within a stone's throw of the top. The remainder of the climb involves 5 m of scrambling up a little wall to a patch of treacherously loose rubble and a precarious summit perch. While the total distance from the top of the gully to the summit is less than 20 m, it is fairly exposed. Part of it is also disconcertingly loose; not a place for beginners.

When I first ascended this peak an inquisitive mountain goat peered down at me from above, watching intently. My slow progress quickly allayed his apprehension, and he casually scampered away, seemingly oblivious to the terrific drop below.

MOUNT MURRAY 3023 m

Difficulty A moderate scramble via north ridge to south-west side
Ascent time 3-6 hours, including ascent of unnamed (Cegnfs)
Height gain 1135 m
Map 82 J/14 Spray Lakes Reservoir
82 J/11 Kananaskis Lakes
(unmarked 205230)

Mount Murray in the rugged French Creek area is a straightforward scramble with the best moment occurring at a brief rockband near the top. An unnamed lesser peak is ascended along the way. Most editions of topo maps do not yet indicate Mount Murray by the road at co-ordinates 205230 (bottom of 82 J/14), and so far this overlooked peak has not seen much activity. Try from July on.

Park at Burstall Pass parking lot on Smith-Dorrien Trail/Spray Lakes Road, 44 km south of Canmore and 20 km north of the Smith-Dorrien Trail/Kananaskis Lakes Trail junction.

From the Burstall Pass parking lot hike the old logging road past Mud Lake. When the trail curves right up the hill, continue straight ahead on an old logging road which soon crosses French Creek and follows the south bank. Upon reaching the first waterfall, leave the valley bottom and hike east through moderate bush. Travel becomes easier as you near open slopes and scree which lead you without difficulty to unnamed (Cegnfs) at 205242.

Descend gentle slopes south to the intervening col and ascend towards Mount Murray, traversing around the north and west sides slightly below steep summit cliffs. The simplest way to surmount this guard-band is by continuing to circle around until close to the south-west ridge. A brief scramble completes the ascent.

On your **return**, numerous unseen bluffs below the Murray-Cegnfs col effectively eliminate a more direct return to the valley. While it is not necessary to plod all the way back up Cegnfs to descend to French Creek, you do have to contour far enough around to outflank rockbands above tree-line meadows.

Mount Murray is named for General Sir A.J. Murray, Chief of the Imperial General Staff, 1915, and General Officer commanding in Egypt 1916-17. Cegnfs is an unlikely acronym derived from the initials of the first ascent party and is entirely unofficial.

MOUNT BURSTALL 2760 m

Difficulty Difficult east ridge scrambling; exposure for final 100 m
Ascent time 2-4 hours
Height gain 900 m
Map 82 J/14 Spray Lakes Reservoir

A quick and simple approach makes this minor summit a logical choice when am-bition, good weather or time is scarce. Close to the road and sheltered by the higher summits of French, Robertson and Sir Douglas, the route up Mount Burstall is straightforward save for the summit ridge where you are obliged to scramble over steeper, more exposed slabs. Try from mid-July on.

Park at Burstall Pass parking lot on Smith-Dorrien Trail/Spray Lakes Road, 44 km south of Canmore and 20 km north of the Smith-Dorrien Trail/Kananaskis Lakes Trail junction.

From the parking lot follow Burstall Pass trail for some 30 minutes. Five minutes beyond a massive boulder lying squarely on the path, head off left up the logged slope to a wide avalanche gully below the east ridge. You gain height quickly here. Upon reaching the broad saddle it is evident where to go — vestiges of sheep trails on the grassy hillside lead up the rubbly terrain of the east ridge to-wards the summit, visible above. The culminating ridge looks nar-row, steep and intimidating. As becomes more apparent, you will be below the airy crest for most of its length.

At one point it appears feasible to cross a broad slab and ascend a long right-angle corner below a large block to gain the ridge crest. It is better, however, to climb straight up a big crack lying left

Photo: Reg Bonney

East ridge route showing S saddle.
C Cegnfs and M Mt. Murray behind.

of this right-angle corner. There are a couple of exposed spots along the ridge crest but they are short. A continuation to the lower west end of the mountain is possible but involves one tricky exposed section at a notch.

Mount Burstall is named for H.E. Burstall, a Canadian Lieutenant-General of World War I.

Opposite: Mt. Murray from Cegnfs. Route skirts summit cliffs to opposite (south-west) side.

MOUNT BULLER 2805 m

Difficulty A moderate scramble via
south-west slopes if upper slabs are
snow-free and dry; exposure
Ascent time 2.5-4.5 hours
Height gain 1000 m
Map 82 J/14 Spray Lakes Reservoir

Mount Buller is close to the road, easily
approached by trail, yet infrequently ascended. This minor Kananaskis peak deserves a visit. Try from June on.

Drive to Buller picnic area on the west
side of Smith-Dorrien Trail/Spray Lakes
Road, 35.4 km south of the Bow River
bridge in Canmore and 32 km north of
the Smith-Dorrien Trail/Kananaskis
Lakes Trail junction.

From the parking area, cross the road
and follow Buller Pass hiking trail for
approximately 30 minutes to a side
stream which drains the south slopes of
Mount Buller. Now leave the Buller Pass
trail and head off to the left along the
bank of this side stream. Continue directly towards a high col visible between
Mount Buller and a subsidiary peak to
the south-west, ascending either lush
green hillside or rockier terrain slightly
to the right. Do not be lured too far right
or you could be in an uncomfortable and
difficult predicament on high steep
slabs. While this portion of the climb is
without difficulty in dry summer conditions, a fatality did occur here one April
and was apparently due to rockfall re-
leased by snow melting.

Once you reach the col (181386) between Buller and the unnamed peak to
the south-west you are two-thirds of the
way there. Now the real toil begins.
Exfoliating slabs peeling off in layers
like an onion skin have created weary-
ing amounts of rubble, giving each
scrambler a chance to prove his resolve.
Over time, much of this debris has completely crumbled into tedious ball-bear-

ing scree. Ski poles would lessen the
misery of this section. Near the top this
peeling effect is particularly evident at
a short, narrow friction slab. Any snow
lingering here will dictate extreme caution due to the airy escarpment on either side. This slab and the accompanying exposure are the chief diversions
from a mostly uneventful march. The
otherwise-pristine summit has been
embellished with a transmitter.

Mount Assiniboine is the reigning
feature to the west; the prominent
pointed peak to its left is Mount Eon
— a summit of historical significance
first ascended in 1921 by Dr. W.E.
Stone, a notable alpinist of the day.
After ascending the upper-most chimney to the summit, he promptly plum-
meted back down it. Waiting close by,
his horrified wife could only watch as
the tragedy occurred.

Speaking of **descents**, the gully draining north from the col can be used to
regain Smith-Dorrien Trail /Spray Lakes
Road, although it is of questionable advantage, unless you fancy a roadside
plod back to your vehicle for a finish.

Henry Cecil Buller was a Lieutenant
in Princess Patricia's Light Infantry
killed in World War I.

*Opposite: Despite its proximity to Spray
Road, Mt. Buller is not a busy place.
B Buller Creek, C col.*

MOUNT ENGADINE 2970 m

Difficulty A difficult scramble via west-
north-west ridge
Ascent time 4-6 hours
Height gain 1170 m
Map 82 J/14 Spray Lakes Reservoir

Mount Engadine is one of the less frequently climbed peaks above the Smith-

Dorrien Trail/Spray Lakes Road, so may
appeal to the recluse. As of 1987, it had
seen but 5 ascents in the previous 16
years. Once you abandon the trail to gain
the west-north-west ridge of the mountain
some tedious bush thrashing ensues. Try
from late June on.

Drive to Buller picnic area on the west
side of Smith-Dorrien Trail/Spray Lakes
Road, 35.4 km south of the Bow River
bridge in Canmore and 32 km north of
the Smith-Dorrien Trail/Kananaskis
Lakes Trail junction.

Cross the road and hike Buller Pass
hiking trail for 15 minutes. Wade or hop
Buller Creek and bushwhack for a half-
hour towards tree-line on the south

side. Walk along the base of high west-
facing slabs signalling the start of the
west-north-west ridge and scramble up
any of several rubbly gullies to gain the
ridge crest.

If you stick to the ridge top, over-
hangs will dictate a couple of easy
detours to the right. Conversely, if you
prefer scree and no exposure, you can
also trudge alongside below, although
this takes the fun out of it. The remain-

Mt. Engadine. Route begins along Buller Creek and ascends ridge. D optional descent route.

Photo: Kris Thorsteinsson

The west-north-west ridge near the summit

der of the route is generally an enjoy-able scramble except for the final 200 m where rock melds into tedious, treadmill rubble. Frustration may well steer you about 100 m to the right where, with luck, a bit of slabby rib should still project above the debris and give better footing.

On **return** we descended this same rubble to the west (much better going down), then continued down broad gul-lies, finally circling around back to the north-west and Buller Creek. It is advis-able to keep fairly high up where slopes are open. This is probably the easiest

means of descent. Another option might be to descend the west-facing gully com-pletely and make a direct line through forest back to the road. It also appears entirely feasible to descend scree on the south side of Mount Engadine to the drainage between it and The Tower to the south-east. The walk out would probably lack a trail.

The Engadine is a world-renowned tourist mecca in the Swiss Alps. How-ever, it is for a ship which played a small part in the Battle of Jutland that this peak is named.

THE TOWER 3117 m

Difficulty A moderate scramble by south-facing scree or snow slopes
Ascent time 3-5 hours
Height gain 1260 m
Map 82 J/14 Spray Lakes Reservoir (unmarked 205351)

In summer, The Tower and its companion valley to the south is one of the most pristine and least-visited spots along the Smith-Dorrien/Spray corridor. Few scramblers have been up this peak, and in spite of its appreciable height, you won't find the name on the topo map. Situated about 1.5 km north-west of Mount Galatea, it has a normal route similar in character to that of Mount Galatea, though not as steep. If there's snow on the route, the glissade descent can be a riot so take an ice-axe. In dry years the peak may be in condition by mid-June, but with a late spring, July would be a more appropriate time.

There are two possible approaches:

Usual Approach

Park on the shoulder of Smith-Dorrien Trail/Spray Lakes Road opposite Mount Shark/Mount Engadine Lodge access road, 7.5 km north of Burstall Pass parking lot and 38.2 km south of Canmore.

From where you've parked, hike south along the old logging road paralleling the highway which begins immediately east of the Mount Shark/Mount Engadine Lodge turn-off. At the first cut block, angle uphill to the left on skid-roads to the upper-most limit of the clearing. Continue through forest until the slope eases, then traverse south-south-east along a semi-open ridge (180330). This ridge becomes better-defined as you go, and you'll have no trouble following Rummel Creek to your left as it curves into the valley. This same route is a popular winter ski trip. Idyllic Rummel Lake is an appropriate place for a break before proceeding past open meadows to the rocky upper valley.

Direct Approach

Park beside the cutline and sign indicating Peter Lougheed Provincial Park boundary on Smith-Dorrien Trail/Spray Lakes Road, 6.7 km north of Burstall Pass parking lot and 39 km south of Canmore.

From the east side of the road head up the cutline. As you cross an old clear-cut where the way becomes ill-defined, continue straight uphill. The cut-line resumes upon entering the forest. Rising steeply, you soon gain the crest of the same ridge traversed by the usual approach. Follow the cutline east down the hillside, across the Rummel Creek, and straight up into Rummel Lake where you join the usual approach route.

Regardless of your approach, resist the temptation to ascend the subsidiary peak west of The Tower. You can't get to the main peak by traversing east, as intervening notches bar the way shortly before the true summit. These notches and the accompanying cliffs will force you to descend almost completely to valley bottom. Instead, wander past Rummel

Lake and start the ascent just beyond the second lake (206336). Clamber up scree slopes which reveal a third and final pond set in a barren bowl to the north-east. Gradually work your way right and over towards the ridge and so to the top.

Confusion surrounds the unofficial name. Historical records show that a climbing party led by Hans Gmoser in 1957 referred to their first ascent as "The Tower", but their photos clearly illustrate a peak known today as "The Fortress" lying 3.5 km to the south-east. Apparently, during the intervening years, the title has migrated to this more northerly mountain. Although it doesn't resemble a tower, the epithet does have a better ring to it than "Unnamed 3117".

The south face of The Tower.

MOUNT CHESTER 3054 m

Difficulty An easy ascent via scree and slabs of south-west side
Ascent time 2.5-4 hours
Height gain 1150 m
Map 82 J/14 Spray Lakes Reservoir

Mount Chester offers pleasant scrambling beginning in alpine meadows near a lake. An excellent return for the effort and a personal favourite of mine. Chester is normally possible from July on.

As a base for scrambling up the adjacent Mounts Galatea, Fortress and Gusty Peak, lush meadows around Chester Lake provide a superb central location. A well-situated camp would make it practical to do two of these peaks in one day — should you be so enthusiastic! If you go, please treat this fragile area with care. Scars from heavy visitor use don't heal quickly in the harsh climate found at this elevation.

Park at Chester Lake parking lot on Smith-Dorrien Trail/Spray Lakes Road, 44 km south of Canmore and 20 km north of the Smith-Dorrien Trail/Kananaskis Lakes Trail junction.

Follow the popular hiking trail to Chester Lake. This path begins as an old logging road and later dwindles to a footpath as it enters forest. Within an hour you emerge into open alpine terrain and larch meadows alongside the stream draining Chester Lake.

Minutes before reaching the lake, cross the creek and wander south across flowery meadows towards the col immediately west of Mount Chester. Hike up the broad gully to the saddle. It is also possible but less direct to gain this col from Headwall Lakes to the south, or to use that valley as an optional exit. During prime season, late July to mid-August, you may discover a profusion of wildflowers eking out a fleeting existence on these harsh slopes. After basking in views of the western sky-

From the summit (left to right) The Tower, Mt. Galatea, Gusty Peak and The Fortress.

line, turn your gaze eastward. Firm, knobby slabs yield a short and enjoyable scramble to the summit 300 m above. Should anyone desire scree, there is plenty of it further right.

The summit panorama rivals that obtained on nearby Mount Galatea, with views of peaks such as Farnham Tower in the Purcell Range 90 km west. Loftier peaks nearby include Mount Assiniboine — the "Matterhorn of the Rockies", Mount Sir Douglas and Mount Joffre, all of which soar to more than 3353 m (11,000'). This vantage point also affords the opportunity to study the equally easy ascent routes for The Fortress and Gusty Peak north-east and north of you, respectively.

Chester, Galatea, Engadine, Indefatigable, Shark and several other peaks in this area borrow their names from cruisers and destroyers involved in the Battle of Jutland, a notable conflict fought during World War I. Its significance is two-fold: it was the only time when both the entire British and German fleets were engaged; furthermore, it ended in a stalemate.

Opposite: Mt. Chester from Smith-Dorrien Trail. G gully, S saddle.

THE FORTRESS 3000 m

Difficulty An easy scramble via south-west ridge
Ascent time 3-5 hours
Height gain 1100 m
Map 82 J/14 Spray Lakes Reservoir

The Fortress is another popular scramble in the idyllic environs of Chester and Headwall Lakes. By combining the two approach options you can effect a loop, visiting entirely different valleys each complete with exquisite alpine lakes. As seen from Highway 40, the towering 600 m north face above Fortress ski area presents a fortress-like appearance. Even the turrets are evident. However, this viewpoint gives no hint of a gentle shoulder leading easily to the top. Try this ascent from July on.

Park at Chester Lake parking lot on Smith-Dorrien Trail/Spray Lakes Road, 44 km south of Canmore and 20 km north of the Smith-Dorrien Trail/Kananaskis Lakes Trail junction.

Headwall Lakes Approach

An approach from Headwall Lakes, though slightly longer, may be the preferred direction. The scree slope leading to The Fortress/Chester col serves better on ascent, while loose rubble on the Chester Lake side makes for a better descent.

The easiest route to Headwall Lakes is via the color-coded ski trails. On the south side of the parking lot, find the ski sign and follow the blue loop. In 1 km turn left onto a road marked blue/yellow, then in less than 1 km keep right at a junction, angling up a long hill flagged with yellow markers. Upon reaching the logged area on a ridge, continue on the yellow road until it fords Headwall Creek. Many people follow the stream to the upper valley from this point. If you continue uphill and look along the edge of the cutblock, a better trail can be found that leads through forest to the first meadow.

Wander further up valley passing two sparkling lakes separated by a waterfall. Continue beyond into the stony upper reaches of the valley and ascend to the The Fortress/Chester col. Although the summit appears close from this point, allow a full hour for the remainder of the climb as there is still some 325 vertical metres to go.

Surmount the summit block easily on the left (north-west) side. Far below the sheer north face lies Fortress Lake with an awe-inspiring amount of atmosphere between the two. Mount Galatea, the dominant peak to the north-west is another pleasant scramble as are adjacent Mount Chester and Gusty Peak to the west and north of you, respectively.

Chester Lake Approach

Hike the well-used trail to Chester Lake as for Mount Chester. Upon reaching Chester Lake follow the shoreline and various trails around to the waterfall and into the upper valley. Initially meadows, mosses and a bubbling stream, this jumbled landscape of boulders becomes increasingly barren as you progress. Shortly before a tiny pond, angle up talus slopes on your right to gain The Fortress/Chester col. Snow often lingers on this shadowy slope and may allow a fast and exciting descent if you've brought along an ice-axe. From the col, the route coincides with that of the Headwall Lakes option.

*The Fortress as seen from the Chester Lake side. C The Fortress/Chester col.
From col the route follows the easy slope to summit block.*

Photo: Gillean Daffern

*Summit view of Mt. Assiniboine, Gusty Peak, Mt. Galatea and The
Tower. Photo shows ascent routes for the latter three peaks.*

MOUNT GALATEA 3185 m

Difficulty A difficult scramble with possibility of steep snow by the south face and ridge
Ascent time 3.5-6 hours
Height gain 1280 m
Map 82 J/14 Spray Lakes Reservoir

Mount Galatea is the finest viewpoint of the Kananaskis Range. Like adjacent summits, it is approached by a popular trail via larch meadows and lakes. Peaks as distant as Mount Olive on the Wapta Icefields and Howser Towers in the Purcell Range can be identified on a clear day, not to mention at least ten of the eighteen peaks over 3350 m scattered around the southern Rockies. The upper section of the route is quite steep, but lower portions make for a good glissade if you have the right snow conditions and an ice-axe. The ascent is more mountaineering than just scrambling, and should be avoided if significant snow lingers on the upper face. Try from late June on.

Park at Chester Lake parking lot on Smith-Dorrien Trail/Spray Lakes Road, 44 km south of Canmore and 20 km north of the Smith-Dorrien Trail/Kananaskis Lakes Trail junction.

Follow the well-used hiking trail to Chester Lake as for Mount Chester. A good trail diverges left along the north shore and leads over a gentle rise into a spectacular valley immediately north of Chester Lake. Continue up valley past two small ponds to an obvious large scree pile at the base of Galatea's south face. Ascend this slope towards a small waterfall. Keep to the right as you ascend, utilizing slabs to reduce some of the treadmilling while also avoiding the fall-line of stones from steadily deteriorating cliffs above.

Higher up, the face meets the south ridge. Follow it as it curves left near the top, moving back onto the face if steps along the ridge present difficulties. It is difficult not to notice the increasing angle of the slope. When dry this is of small consequence. If snow-clad, as it often is in June, it feels a little uncomfortable even with an ice-axe to be out on this steep incline once the sun begins to soften the snow. Use caution here. After a two hour plod uphill, however, the rapid ten minute glissade back down should be memorable if not apprehensive. In spite of its commanding height, the peak doesn't see too many visitors.

The summit of Mount Galatea boasts far-ranging vistas and many happy hours could be spent here attempting to identify surrounding as well as distant mountains. For those interested in doing The Tower (3117 m) immediately north, no better viewpoint exists for surveying the line of ascent. Once the wind comes up and the Kananaskis rock has made a suitable impression on you, return the same way.

Galatea was a British cruiser engaged in the historic World War I Battle of Jutland; in mythology, her role as a beautiful sea-nymph was a decidedly less militaristic one.

The south face of Mt. Galatea is a good glissade in the right conditions.

GUSTY PEAK 3000 m

Difficulty An easy ascent via
south scree slopes
Ascent time 3-5 hours
Height gain 1100 m
Map 82 J/14 Spray Lakes Reservoir
(unmarked 227322)

Gusty Peak, located near scenic Chester Lake is perched between The Fortress and Mount Galatea. As of summer '89 it had only been ascended three times. Despite being ignored by the hordes who favour nearby Mount Chester, the view is respectable and the ascent straightforward. Try from July on.

Park at Chester Lake parking lot on Smith-Dorrien Trail/Spray Lakes Road, 44 km south of Canmore and 20 km north of the Smith-Dorrien Trail/Kananaskis Lakes Trail junction.

Follow the hiking trail to Chester Lake as described for Mount Chester. Upon reaching the lake, continue north-east into the upper valley as for The Fortress almost as far as The Fortress/Chester col. Here you should be right by the west shore of a tiny pond. Facing north, angle diagonally up to your right on scree slopes of the objective. Because the true summit lies at the easternmost end of the uplift and not directly above, you are advised to follow the bedding angle of the strata. It ramps directly summit-ward. The foreshortened view directly above has misled some people (including the author) into thinking the highest point may be straight up. In fact, charging up this line only leads to increasingly steep terrain and the lower west summit of Gusty Peak. Traversing east along the connecting ridge to the true summit is distasteful.

Assuming it's free of snow, this south-facing route is little more than a stiff walk up and back down a rocky slope. The only stumbling blocks you are likely to encounter will be of the limestone variety. This rubble is com-

posed chiefly of the Banff Formation, a geological rock unit of some 360 million years ago prevalent throughout the Front Ranges. It often contains horn coral fossils — which look just like the name suggests. Ramblers in the eastern Rockies frequently unearth more of this fossil than any other type.

Gusty Peak is the unofficial label given by the first ascent party in 1972 who went up this nondescript lump of limestone in less than perfect summer conditions of snow and high winds.

The straightforward south scree slopes.
W west summit.

BANFF AND THE BOW VALLEY

Mount Inglismaldie	2964 m	moderate	p. 112
Mount Aylmer	3163 m	easy	p. 114
Cascade Mountain	2998 m	moderate	p. 116
Mount Rundle	2949 m	easy	p. 118
Mount Norquay	2522 m	moderate	p. 120
Mount Edith	2554 m	moderate	p. 122
Mount Cory	2802 m	easy	p. 125
Mount Bourgeau	2930 m	easy	p. 126
Pilot Mountain	2935 m	difficult	p. 128
Mount Brett	2984 m	difficult	p. 129
Copper Mountain	2795 m	moderate	p. 130
Castle Mountain	2766 m	easy	p. 131
Stuart Knob	2850 m	easy	p. 132
Helena Ridge	2862 m	easy	p. 133
Television Peak	2970 m	easy	p. 134
Mount Whymper	2845 m	moderate	p. 135
Storm Mountain	3161 m	moderate	p. 136
Mount Ball	3311 m	moderate	p. 138

This chapter covers peaks adjacent to Banff townsite and as far west along the Trans-Canada Highway as Castle Junction. This junction, some 30 km from Banff, is where Highway 93 from Radium, B.C. intersects. A few scrambles in Kootenay National Park at the northern end of Banff-Radium Highway have also been included in this section. Some of the Rockies' most photographed mountains grace the horizon in this area, mountains like Mount Rundle, Cascade and Castle Mountain. Many, including these famous three, are scrambles.

Banff National Park is the most visited of the four contiguous mountain parks, with Banff townsite bearing the brunt of the traffic. As you might suspect, backcountry areas are similarly well-used. As all the scrambles in this chapter can be done in one long day from a vehicle, (one *very* long day to do Mount Ball), crowded backcountry campsites will be of no concern.

Most of this section of the Rockies is still within the Front Ranges, and not until Castle Mountain do you reach the Main Ranges. With its castellated towers and soaring buttresses, the change in topography is startling. Main Ranges are old, the oldest in the Rockies, and date back 600-800 million years. Most of the highest peaks are found here.

Unless west of the Continental Divide, underbrush is of little consequence on approaches, but areas west of Banff are nonetheless wetter than those to the east. Snow leaves the alpine meadows slowly. June is normally the wettest of summer months in the mountains. There are also periodic snow dumps at higher elevations, and eager mountain enthusiasts sometimes experience feelings of hopelessness about summer's slow progression. Patience is the key. Invariably, better weather does show up, but you never know how long it will stay! Historically, the most stable period of summer weather usually occurs near the end of July and the first week of August. September and October usually grant a prolonged dry spell or two, but temperatures are much cooler and higher peaks may be snowy again by that time.

Access Banff sits alongside the Trans-Canada Highway, 1.5 hours drive west of Calgary. To stop in National Parks requires a permit; these are sold at entrance gates. The other major road within the Park is Bow Valley Parkway (1-A Highway) which begins 6 km west of Banff and runs for 30 km along the north side of the Bow Valley to Castle Junction. Kootenay Parkway (Highway 93) intersects the Trans-Canada at Castle Junction and leads south-west to Radium, B.C.

Facilities For those snubbed by mercurial weather, Banff has everything you could want — crowds included. You can find anything you need in the way of maps, gear, food, entertainment and information. After a tiring slog, the Cave and Basin Hot pools on Sulphur Mountain are a welcome respite. Gear-wise, ice-axes and crampons can be rented at Performance Ski and Sports and at Mountain Magic. Monod's Sports and Mountain Magic also carry a full line of outdoor supplies.

West of Banff, there is a small, congenial store and gas station at Castle Junction, and a cafe at Johnston Canyon on the 1-A. Meals are available at Storm Mountain Lodge on Highway 93.

Accommodation Tunnel Mountain Campground is located close to Banff townsite, as is the co-ed YWCA. A variety of other accommodation exists in the vicinity — mostly expensive. Farther west are additional campgrounds along 1-A Highway, also at Marble Canyon on Highway 93 in Kootenay Park. Castle Junction offers a youth hostel and bungalows. Other lodging can be found at Johnston Canyon, Baker Creek and Storm Mountain Lodge. Don't depend on being able to show up and find room though. Like the campgrounds, all these places fill up fast. If nothing else, there is a big, ugly gravel pit on the Trans-Canada east of Lake Louise called "Lake Louise Overflow". Many latecomers end up settling there for the night.

Information Parks Canada's bustling Information Centre is at 224 Banff Avenue. Just look for an assortment of souls poring over maps and brochures along the sidewalk. In Kootenay Park, watch for a small building at Marble Canyon, 7 km west of Castle Junction.

Wardens The Banff Warden Office is located just east of the townsite on the north side of Banff Avenue at the Parks Compound. Specific information about current mountain conditions can often be obtained here.

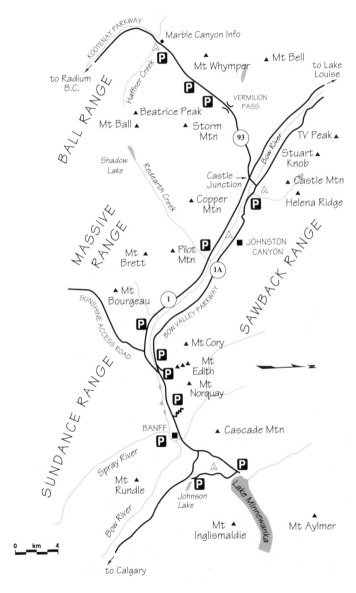

to Radium B.C.

KOOTENAY PARKWAY

Marble Canyon Info

Haffner Creek

BALL RANGE

▲ Mt Whymper

▲ Mt Bell

to Lake Louise

VERMILION PASS

▲ Beatrice Peak

Mt Ball ▲

▲ Storm Mtn

93

Bow River

TV Peak ▲

Stuart ▲ Knob

Shadow Lake

Redearth Creek

Castle Junction

▲ Castle Mtn

Helena Ridge

MASSIVE RANGE

▲ Copper Mtn

JOHNSTON CANYON

Mt ▲ Brett

▲ Pilot Mtn

1A

SUNSHINE ACCESS ROAD

▲ Mt Bourgeau

1

BOW VALLEY PARKWAY

SAWBACK RANGE

▲ Mt Cory

Mt Edith

Mt Norquay

BANFF

▲ Cascade Mtn

Spray River

Mt Rundle

Johnson Lake

Lake Minnewanka

Bow River

Mt ▲ Inglismaldie

▲ Mt Aylmer

0 km 4

to Calgary

SUNDANCE RANGE

111

MOUNT INGLISMALDIE 2964 m

Difficulty A moderate scramble
via south-west slopes
Ascent time 5-8 hours
Height gain 1450 m
Map 82 O/3 Canmore

Although Mount Inglismaldie rewards
the victorious with fine views of Lake
Minnewanka and the Bow Corridor, it
sees little activity due to lack of an approach trail. As you drive towards Banff
from the west, this peak, along with
adjacent Mount Girouard to the south,
form a balanced and symmetrical backdrop on the eastern horizon. Were there
a good trail, it would likely be as popular
as nearby Rundle or Cascade. Try from
late June on.

South-west slopes of Inglismaldie. D alternative descent.

Less than perfect weather on Mt. Inglismaldie

From Banff east overpass, follow Lake Minnewanka Road for 5 km past the Cadet Camp to Johnson Lake.

From the parking area at Johnson Lake skirt north to avoid a large boggy area feeding the lake, then wander through pine forest aiming to pick up the drainage between Girouard and Inglismaldie. Along the way you will probably pass remnants of two collapsed log cabins. Early in summer the creek is fairly sizeable, dictating numerous bothersome crossings. Tempting as it may be, avoid climbing too high above the creek — cliffs will make it difficult to descend further upstream. After some three hours, you reach the upper limits of the drainage where it forks. By heading right, you can readily gain the base of a long slope of good scree facing generally south-west. This is the easiest way up. More panoramic and distant scenes unfold to the west as you hike up this easy slope while nearby, Mount Girouard looms silently, inviting speculation as to its ease of ascent.

Towards the top, rockbands block upward progress, necessitating a traverse left over scree and slabby ledges to finish with a direct line to the summit. Appreciably steeper on the east, Inglismaldie grants excellent views including a fine perspective of lengthy Lake Minnewanka and a daunting view of Devil's Head to the north.

As an **alternative descent**, the entire face directly below the summit can be descended without much problem. As studied from the Banff east overpass this face appears quite steep. However, only a few short rock steps require detours. With good snow conditions and an ice-axe this line can make for a rapid glissade descent, depositing you a short way along the left or north branch of the drainage forks.

Upon occasion of the Earl of Kintore's visit in 1886 or '87, George A. Stewart, Superintendent of Rocky Mountains Park (later Banff Park) named the peak for Inglismaldie Castle in Kincardineshire, Scotland. This locality was the seat of the Earl of Kintore.

MOUNT AYLMER 3163 m

Difficulty An easy ascent via southwest slopes
Ascent time 2.5-5 hours
Height gain 1680 m
Map 82 O/6 Lake Minnewanka

Mount Aylmer is Banff's highest mountain and one of the more prominent points in The Front Ranges. Much of the mountain is obscured by southern ramparts of The Palliser Range, but the lofty summit does manage to project enough to be noticed nonetheless. Despite the long trek, numerous parties make the ascent each season, some camping at the nearby campsite — entirely unnecessarily. For a day trip a mountain bike is invaluable though sections of path are rough and rooty. Some years the ascent is possible by mid-June, but as frequently, a cold spring rain will deposit inches of snow on the upper flanks and delay ascents for a week or more. Fortunately, this snow-prone section is visible near the Banff east overpass, so you need not rush off blindly.

From Banff east overpass on the Trans-Canada Highway drive east along Lake Minnewanka Road for 5.5 km to the Lake Minnewanka Concession Area. Park here.

From the parking lot, walk or bike past the concession stand, the picnic tables and the washrooms. Follow the lake shore trail for 7.6 km to the campsite at Aylmer Pass cut-off, an agreeable spot on the shore of Lake Minnewanka well suited to nibbling and filling water bottles. This is as far as bicycles can be ridden. All is uphill and on foot beyond here, and to add to the toil, you have gained not a whit of elevation yet.

Suitably rejuvenated, follow the signed Aylmer Pass/Aylmer Lookout path uphill of the campsite. Upon reaching a fork in this path you have a choice. The right branch, which leads to the site of Aylmer fire lookout, adds distance through some unnecessarily long switchbacks but works well otherwise. From the old lookout site proceed north along the ridge. The way is obvious. The left fork to Aylmer Pass is a more pleasant route, gradually rising amid semi-open forest. Follow this until you emerge into the open in a large avalanche gully; about one hour of fast walking. The hiking path crosses the gully and angles steeply to the left. Scramblers heading for Mount Aylmer will want to forego the trail at this point and instead hike up this twisting gully onto the hillside above near a minor bump of brown scree. The route from Aylmer Lookout joins where you gain the crest of the slope. Both routes could

Mt. Aylmer from north of the old fire lookout. Aylmer Pass route ascends left skyline.

be incorporated to add variety on return. Continue along this ridge as it sweeps around to the right towards the summit. The highest section of the ridge has been formed by uplifted strata resulting in three short rockbands, two of which are heavily eroded. The middle one requires a short scramble down a 5 m crack. Now you have at last reached the final talus slope leading to the summit — a good place to take a breather and admire the surroundings before starting the final skyward plod. A good trail rises in zigzags but serves better on descent than ascent. Ski-poles help here. As you top out, be aware of the summit cornice which often partially obstructs the easterly vista.

Views are pleasing but hardly stunning. Much of the panorama appears as nameless piles of brown rubble, although green hues of Upper Ghost River and the meadows beyond Aylmer Pass

make a valiant effort to ease the monotonous lack of color. Due to the southwesterly dip-slope bedding of Front Range peaks, the eastern aspects of these mountains are usually most impressive. A glance across the lake at Mounts Inglismaldie, Girouard and Peechee tends to bolster this supposition.

There are a few theories regarding the name. A popular one suggests that J. J. McArthur, a Dominion Land Surveyor named the peak for his home town in Quebec. Since it was he who made the first ascent in 1889, this explanation would seem most plausible.

It would appear that Aylmer is the mountain known as "Spirit Mountain" of Assiniboine Indian legend. Lake Minnewanka or "Water of the Spirits" was believed to be home to a half-fish half-human creature, and, until Whites arrived, Indians superstitiously avoided fishing or canoeing the waters.

Opposite: Mt. Aylmer as seen from Sulphur Mtn. showing the final section of the route.

CASCADE MOUNTAIN 2998 m

Difficulty Moderate scrambling
via west and south slopes
Ascent time 3.5-5.5 hours
Height gain 1325 m
Map 82 O/4 Banff

Cascade Mountain is one of two Banff classics, the other being Mount Rundle, which should be on any scramblers list of peaks. Since the first ascent in 1887 by Tom Wilson and partner, hundreds of happy hoofers have trudged up this popular peak. Decades ago, a couple of ambitious Banff residents carefully toted a mirror to the top and strategically erected it to reflect down Banff Avenue during summer months, although all traces of the endeavour have since been lost to time.

In an entertaining account of an early ascent of Cascade, Canmore writer Ralph Connor claimed to have stumbled upon "the fossil remains of a prehistoric monster". Due to the incredible weight of the find, he explained, they "left them behind us, and they are there to this day for some anthropologist to see". Modern day adventurers are unlikely to uncover any fragment of this figment during their ascent, and will have to be satisfied with ever-improving views or perhaps the occasional curious rock formation along the way. Try from July on.

From Banff west overpass on the Trans-Canada Highway drive north up the winding Norquay Ski Area access road for 6 km. Park in #1 parking lot on the right next to Cascade daylodge.

From the north end of the parking lot, walk past Cascade daylodge and follow the signed Cascade Amphitheatre hiking trail as it descends to cross Forty Mile Creek. When the path forks be sure to take the right branch and continue up innumerable switchbacks into Cascade Amphitheatre. From this grassy glade, the roving eye falls on a gently-angled ridge sweeping skyward from right to left towards Cascade's barren summit, 800 vertical metres above. It is this ridge

Photo: Don Beers

Cascade Mtn. from Sulphur Mountain. F false summit.

which blesses the scrambler with a feasible and well frequented means of attaining those arid heights.

Various trails departing the meadow's edge quickly head ridge-ward. Patches of Mountain Sorrel grow hereabouts, the tart flavour of which is reminiscent of domestic rhubarb and can help alleviate thirst. Above tree-line, unimpeded views of the Bow Corridor make the confined amphitheatre seem almost claustrophobic by comparison.

The only obstacle en route is the false summit, visible as a big bump along the ridge when viewed from the highway. There are two ways of dealing with it. Either climb down over its south side, which is what most people end up doing, or skirt around the west end and

Opposite: The summit ridge is clearly seen above Cascade Amphitheatre. Route gains ridge at right of picture.

south side. You will probably end up backtracking as you typically don't notice that you're on the false summit until beyond the detour point. Snow tends to linger along the foot of this minor eminence into July. The terrain is rather slabby, smooth and entirely unpleasant when snowy so it is well worth determining beforehand from the highway whether this unavoidable bit is "in condition", or the trek could be for naught.

Cascade is Dr. James Hector's abbreviated translation of an Indian name for the peak, and depicts the familiar waterfall which so mysteriously emerges from barren rock high upon the south flanks. Coincidentally, this scholarly member of the Palliser expedition labelled a host of nearby landmarks, including Mounts Rundle and Bourgeau.

MOUNT RUNDLE 2949 m

Difficulty An easy scramble
via west slopes
Ascent time 3-5 hours
Height gain 1570 m
Map 82 O/4 Banff

Mount Rundle is arguably the most popular scramble in Banff vicinity, if not in all of Banff National Park. It is an easily recognized peak, presenting a classic example of a dip-slope or writing-desk geological formation, particularly when seen from the west. When snow-free there are only minor difficulties involved in ascending the gentle, west slope which gives an excellent view of Bow Valley and Vermilion Lakes. Over the years, though, this appealing mountain has provided its quota of call-outs for Parks rescue personnel. The windswept normal route often comes into shape fairly early in the year; try from May on.

In Banff, drive along Spray Avenue. Before reaching Banff Springs Hotel turn left and drive down to Banff Springs Golf Course. Cross Spray River bridge and 0.4 km past the first green take the dirt road heading right through the first green. Park at a gate 0.5 km farther on.

From the parking spot, go through the gate and hike along the gravel road for five minutes, watching for the signed hiking trail branching left. This beaten path rises gently through pine and fir forest typical of eastern slope valleys throughout the Rockies. Before long, numerous switchbacks grind their way steadily upwards past a directional sign indicating the lower first peak. Ignore this and continue straight ahead. Some 10 to 20 minutes beyond this point is where many people go wrong.

The trail emerges into a sizeable watercourse which reveals lofty heights far above, and it is here where a significant number of persons have blindly chosen to charge straight up this slabby, ever-steepening chute. By contrast, the normal and easier route lies almost directly across this typically dry channel, re-entering forest instead. The way is marked by conspicuous stripes of blue and white paint on trees and rocks. Any number of paths wend hastily upwards and finally emerge onto slab and talus of the west face at tree-line. The route is obvious and easy if dry, but note the escarpment on your left. For a short distance the way is slabby and only about one to two metres wide. Both sides drop-off, but it isn't very exposed and there shouldn't be a problem.

The last few hundred metres are especially wearisome, mocking the most concerted efforts at forward progress — rubble without a pause. If ever there was a place to try ski-poles on scree, this is it. On a hot summer day, when heat waves shimmer off barren rock and create mirages of much-needed but non-existent water, you'll be glad of simple things like refreshments, a hat and a good pair of sunglasses.

For anyone contemplating a traverse over to the first peak, it is much more difficult and exposed. A rope and knowledge of its use are recommended. It is **NOT** a scramble.

Mount Rundle is named for the Reverend Robert Rundle, a Wesleyan missionary and early "tourist" to Banff. Although he never actually attempted the peak, it appears he almost reached the top of one farther east, the location of which is unrecorded.

W

Mt. Rundle. W watercourse

MOUNT NORQUAY 2522 m

Difficulty Moderate scrambling; awkward for 5-10 m; brief exposure
Ascent time 3.5-6 hours
Height gain 1000 m from bottom of lift, 600 m from top of lift
Map 82 O/4 Banff

Mount Norquay is an ideal site to scope out Mounts Louis, Rundle and Cascade. For those detesting the inevitable hard work but still hoping to "bag" a summit, this outing may be the answer. Sacrilegious though it may be, cheaters can even ride the lift, if it's running, saving half the total elevation gain. Try from mid-June on.

From Banff west overpass on the Trans-Canada Highway drive north up the winding Norquay Ski Area access road for 6 km. Continue past Cascade daylodge and park in the lot near the older Norquay daylodge at the base of the ski runs.

From the daylodge at the base of the hill, use your chosen mode of transportation to reach the upper terminal of the Norquay lift. Look for a good trail leaving the right rear (north) corner of the upper terminal building and follow it as it lazily angles across two large gullies to gain a small promontory on a ridge by a stand of larches. The path now heads back left up this ridge to the foot of a steep wall. A rather exposed slabby scramble, entirely unpleasant if wet, leads to an old repeater tower on a shoulder of Mount Norquay above. There is room for variation here; you may find it preferable to skirt the steep wall to the right and work your way up low-angled slabs beside a short gully. Above that, head left to reach the tower.

Another route of ascent, more direct but perhaps marginally more demanding as well, would be to scramble up in a fairly straight line from the right rear corner of the upper terminal building. Look for a shallow, right-trending gully leading upwards to the ridge above.

Once you top out at the tower, it will become clear that in spite of having achieved a respectable survey spot you are still some distance from the true summit lying farther west. What's more, there appears to be a deep intervening valley! Don't despair. A high saddle actually connects to that apparently remote summit mass but lies just out of sight.

Continue north along the airy ridge — the crux is at hand. A short corner provides a bit of challenge up to a large platform and a cairn slightly further on. This affords an opportunity to scope out the remaining section. Once they do, some people decide to remain here. The continuation starts as a mere stroll, then, where the connecting ridge abuts against the main summit block, you must angle to the right over ledges and scree, following the bedding of the strata for a short distance. The route tops out slightly north of the register.

Perhaps the most striking scene lies north towards Mounts Louis and Edith, their near-vertical dogtooth strata thrusting skyward. Sharp eyes and binoculars often discern climbers on the steep popular south face of Louis, a prized addition to any climber's collection of accomplishments. Although ascended regularly, Mount Louis even today continues to record an impressive roster of souls who, for various reasons, have

been forced into unplanned bivouacs —
an occurrence which speaks volumes for
Albert MacCarthy and Conrad Kains'
uneventful first ascent in 1916.

Assuming you arrive back in time,
you may be lucky enough to obtain a
free ride down the gondola, and it is
entirely ethical to accept.

As an **alternative descent** from the
west summit, scramble down the south
ridge which meets the Trans-Canada
Highway about 3 km west of the west
overpass. Chief difficulties are scaling
the fence by the road and getting a lift
back to your car.

Mount Norquay commemorates The
Honourable John Norquay, popular Pre-
mier of Manitoba from 1878-87 who apparently made the ascent during his term
in office and did not use the gondola.

*Route to west summit from saddle
between east and west peaks.*

The east side of Mt. Norquay, showing two routes to the east summit.
E east summit, W west (true) summit, S saddle connecting the two summits, D alternative descent.

Photo: Bruno Engler

MOUNT EDITH 2554 m

Difficulty North and Centre peaks moderate scrambling from Cory Pass; South Peak difficult from centre/south col with some exposure
Ascent time 3.5-5 hours
Height gain 1120 m
Map 82 O/4 Banff

Mount Edith consists of three separate summits of varying difficulty approached by a popular hiking trail. A dogtooth mountain like its northerly and more famous neighbour Mount Louis, Mount Edith is an uplift of Devonian age Palliser limestone — a 500 m-thick formation of sound rock prevalent throughout the Rockies. Palliser rock forms great grey cliffs on many mountains, but fortunately does not present a significant deterrent in this instance. In fact, the north and central peaks require few technical climbing skills. Try this outing from June on.

From Banff west overpass drive west along the Trans-Canada Highway to Bow Valley Parkway. 0.3 km along Bow Valley Parkway turn right and follow the access road to Fireside Picnic Site and Cory/Edith Pass trailhead.

North & Centre Peaks

Follow the 6 km-long Cory Pass trail (go left at the fork) to within a few minutes of Cory Pass, whereupon a path leads in an easterly direction up scree towards North Peak (highest) 200 m above. The top is guarded by a belt of cliffs, but on the north-west side a short chimney cleaves this band and will undoubtedly provide interesting moments as you wriggle up it. The striking obelisk of Mount Louis can be scrutinized at close quarters from this perspective.

It is a straightforward 20-minute scramble to the slightly lower Centre Peak. At the time of writing both summits boast a register.

Centre Peak can be descended easily via a scree gully on the south side towards the south peak and Cory Pass trail.

Going up or down? The chimney on North Peak provides entertaining scrambling.

Photo: Don Beers

South peak and Centre/South col from Centre peak. G ascent gully. Cory Pass trail below to right.

Top: Centre peak from North peak — no problems involved. Note South Peak behind.

Centre peak from the Centre/South col, showing easy descent gully..

South Peak

The south peak is much more demanding and exposed than either the north or centre peaks. Confident scramblers with good route-finding skills who ideally are undeterred by exposure can ascend the climbers descent route on the airy west side.

The route begins slightly below the centre/south col on the west side in a north-facing gully. It can also be accessed from the Cory Pass trail by ascending the scree slope towards the col.

Starting innocently enough, it ascends a gully for about 5-8 m, then dodges around to the right on an exposed ledge. Rather than use this ledge, there is also the option of a claustrophobic, dirty tunnel for average-sized and smaller folks to crawl through. As you can see, the route has something for everyone. These features are the keys to starting the route. Cairns found at intervals beyond are mildly re-assuring, but the route is meandering and exposed in several places. Wrong variations are worse.

Depending on your line, you may top out either slightly north or south of the cairn. Although elevation gain from the col is a trivial 100 vertical metres, the ascent may rank as the most stressful of any in this guide. Take careful note of your ascent route for the return.

Descent Regardless of whether or not you include South Edith on your itinerary, you can readily regain Cory Pass trail from centre/south col between south and centre summits. Stumble down scree, watching for the beaten path well to your right at the base of a wall. This avoids slabby downsloping steps in the middle of the gully directly below.

Edith Orde accompanied Lady Agnes MacDonald, wife of Canada's first Prime Minister, on her 1886 journey through the Rockies by the newly-completed transcontinental railway, in the process lending her name to the mountain.

North, Centre and South Peaks (left to right). Route to C and S peaks shown.

Photo: Don Beers

MOUNT CORY 2802 m

Difficulty An easy scramble
via south ridge
Ascent time 4-6 hours
Height gain 1370 m
Map 82 O/4 Banff

Mount Cory is a straightforward scramble which grants respectable views. When viewed from the Trans-Canada Highway two notable features distinguish Mount Cory: a 300 m vertical groove climbers call "Cory Crack" which cleaves the southwest face, and a gaping, dark cavern in a slabby face to the right of Cory Crack known as "Hole in the Wall". Most visits centre around these lower flanks which offer several technically difficult rock-climbing routes on high quality limestone.

On the south side of the peak are three parallel treed ribs rising to half the mountain's total height and separated by drainage gullies. The right-hand rib is the straightforward line of ascent, identified by light-coloured, shaly bluffs at the bottom and a deep ravine to the right. The route is often feasible from mid-June on.

Follow Bow Valley Parkway west of Banff for 1.9 km to a pull-off spot. The route begins here.

The pull-off spot sits at the base of this rib. As you wander up through scrub forest you may be lucky enough to glimpse mountain goat which sometimes frequent the environs. The rib eases to a small plateau further up — an ideal lunch spot from which to survey the Bow Corridor.

A further two hours plod up the ridge to the north guides you to the more southerly of Mount Cory's two equally-high summits. The north peak is easily reached after a few more minutes, although a cornice sometimes impedes early season visits. **Descend** by the same route.

Like so many mountains in the Rockies, Mount Cory, in typical bureaucratic tradition, exalts another politician. William Cory was Deputy Minister of the Interior during 1905-1930.

The long south ridge of Mt. Cory leads to a double summit.
Photo: Bruno Engler

MOUNT BOURGEAU 2930 m

Difficulty An easy scramble
via west ridge
Ascent time 4-6 hours
Height gain 1500 m
Map 82 O/4 Banff

Bourgeau Lake is a well-trodden Banff area day hike which provides an easy albeit long approach route to the summit of Mount Bourgeau. The peak was first ascended in 1890 by surveyor J.J. McArthur and packer Tom Wilson, al-though they probably did not use this exact approach. The route frequented to-day visits no less than three distinctly unique mountain tarns along the way and is one of the more congenial undertakings in the Banff area. This area records heavy precipitation. With an ice-axe, early summer enthusiasts can often find lingering snow patches near the second lake on which to practice self-arrest techniques, while also having serious fun glissading. Try from late June on.

Park at Bourgeau Lake parking lot on the south-west side of the Trans-Canada Highway 2.9 km north of Sunshine Ski Area access road turn-off.

From the parking area, follow the hiking trail for 7.5 km to Bourgeau Lake. Upon reaching this clear body of water, follow any of the paths down the right-hand side towards the west end and the inlet stream. To reach the high alpine basin lying west at 835655, the easiest course is to hike along the right side of this rushing brook. Replete with picturesque tarns and meadows, the glacially-carved cirque is far more attractive than Bourgeau Lake itself, yet the majority of people never see it. Continue to Harvey

Looking back down the ridge. The snow-capped peak to right is Mt. Ball.

Pass, the low saddle to the south near tiny Harvey Lake (838651) which reveals expansive views of alpine meadows and, beyond the scars of Sunshine ski area, magnificent Mount Assiniboine. More importantly though, for the scrambler, this pass lies at the foot of Bourgeau's gentle west ridge.

A pleasant walk takes you to Bourgeau's broad summit 400 m higher. Loose scree is practically non-existent on this slope where a surprising quantity of delicate wildflowers bloom throughout much of the summer. In complete contrast to the pastoral panorama, assorted man-made paraphernalia including a building, crowns the top. Despite these intrusions there is plenty of room for wan-

dering the expansive summit plateau. Mount Ball is the hulking snowcapped peak directly to the west, while to the north 350 million years of erosion have sculpted the Sawback Range into long, vertically-tilted rock ridges known as Sawtooth mountains.

The peak was named by James Hector of the Palliser expedition for Monsieur Eugene Bourgeau, the botanist who accompanied the mission on explorations through the Rockies during 1857-60. Highly esteemed in scientific circles, Bourgeau quickly won the admiration of his fellow expedition members during their travels.

Opposite: The gentle west ridge of Mt. Bourgeau rises above ice-bound Harvey Lake. The photo also shows the approach route from Bourgeau Lake (bottom left).

PILOT MOUNTAIN 2935 m

Difficulty Two difficult steps
via north-west ridge; some exposure
Ascent time 4.5-7 hours
Height gain 1535 m
Map 82 O/4 Banff

Pilot Mountain is a striking Bow Valley land-mark that requires a degree of perseverance and route-finding beyond that of other Banff area scrambles. There is no pleasant path delivering you to the heights, and as a result, few have made the ascent over the years despite its proximity to a busy highway. A reasonable access route does exist. For early season outings an ice-axe is suggested; try from late June on.

Park at Redearth Creek parking lot on the south side of the Trans-Canada Highway, 19.6 km west of Banff west overpass and 10.7 km east of Castle Junction. Mountain biking permitted.

From the parking area, bike or hike Redearth Fireroad to the first avalanche slope (one hour on foot), then bid adieu to this perfectly good trail. Wander up the brushy incline in the company of a bubbling stream towards a north-west facing basin carved in Pilot Mountain's lower flanks. It is worth studying the approaching rockband for the most promising line through it as there is more than one potential route. This will simplify route-finding once you've actually got your nose up against the rock.

Pilot Mtn. from Copper Mtn., showing route from Redearth Creek Fireroad. C chimney

Once past this rockband and onto the rubble above, keep traversing right (south) on the open sidehill below an impenetrable wall of smooth limestone until you reach the north-west ridge. At this spot the elements have conveniently eroded this barrier into mere rubble — so much for impenetrable. Scree leads to cliffs and a ten to fifteen metre-high chimney behind a huge detached flake, a logical weakness to assail. On an ascent in early June one year, this big groove still harboured residual snow and ice, and in these conditions it may well require an ice-axe and perhaps even crampons. Lacking the hardware, some wide leg-spreads and bridging maneuverers may suffice depending on your leg length. At the top, move horizontally left on a ledge to easier, less exposed terrain and scramble higher. Just below the top, two short but steep walls constitute the crux. A walk then leads to the broad summit plateau. Persons wishing to ascend Copper Mountain to the north-west have an ideal view of the route up which is also a scramble.

As an **alternative descent** route, or to bag nearby Mount Brett (2984 m), you can drop down into the seldom-visited glen south-west of Pilot Mountain. Retrace your steps to the bottom of the chimney at the base of the north-west ridge, then angle down west-facing rubble slopes where brief rockbands deliver you into this pristine valley. To reach Redearth Fireroad from here, follow the faint, bushy gully north-west.

Mount Brett Option

While the unsavoury loss of hard-won elevation down the rubbly west slopes of Pilot Mountain may have been tiring, continuing to Mount Brett 700 m above will surely drain any remaining energy. Cross the glen and hike up through subalpine forest onto the broad, larch-dotted ridge bordering this rocky vale. Pleasant walking ensues as you wander towards the north-west ridge. Moderate scrambling along the ridge crest gives ready access to the summit which probably sees fewer ascents than does Pilot Mountain.

On **descent**, low-angle rubble on the west slopes of Brett allow a quick descent from the summit. Contour back around to regain the larch-dotted ridge once again. Combining these two scrambles guarantees a long day, but for anyone having aspirations of climbing Mount Brett this combination will save future approaches, none of which is brief.

Pilot Mountain's familiar outline kept early travellers in the Bow Corridor on course and was named accordingly. Doctor R.G. Brett at one time ran the Sanatorium Hotel in Banff, was active in politics and later became Lieutenant-Governor of Alberta, 1915-25.

Typical terrain on the NW ridge of Mt. Brett.

COPPER MOUNTAIN 2795 m

Difficulty A moderate scramble
from Redearth Creek
Ascent time 3-5 hours
Height gain 1375 m
Map 82 O/4 Banff

Hundreds of hikers utilize Redearth Fireroad en route to Egypt and Shadow Lakes but few parties give Copper Mountain much more than a sideways glance. It is not a major summit, neither is it a major undertaking nor a major concern. In 1986 the register bore no record of any visits during the previous fourteen years. To break this unwarranted cycle, try from mid-June on.

Park at Redearth Creek parking lot on the south side of the Trans-Canada Highway, 19.6 km west of Banff west overpass and 10.7 km east of Castle Junction. Mountain biking permitted.

From the parking lot, hike or bike 7.2 km up Redearth Fireroad to Lost Horse campsite. Follow game trails downstream and gain open avalanche slopes immediately to the right (north) of the obvious looming rock face. Hike up these avalanche slopes towards the gully system directly below the summit. Vegetation gives way to easy scrambling and — as you would suspect — the top. The landscape is dominated by a unique view of the long, curving bastion of Castle Mountain which was partially ascended by explorer James Hector and named as early as 1858.

As an **alternate descent route**, a wide shaly gully at the south end of the broad summit provides a quick way back to the fireroad, emerging a short distance upstream of the campsite.

Copper Mountain is named for ore deposits discovered in the area at one time by prospector Joe Healy.

Copper Mtn from Pilot Mtn. Route ascends gullies above tree-line.

CASTLE MOUNTAIN 2766 m

Difficulty An easy scramble
via north-east side
Ascent time 3-6 hours
Height gain 1300 m
Map 82 O/5 Castle Mountain

Castle Mountain has caught the imagination of Bow Valley visitors since man's earliest presence. Although it looks steep and intimidating from the road, it is easily ascended from the back side. The approach is a pleasant and popular hike. When James Hector sighted the mountain in 1858, he noted its suggestive appearance and named it accord-

ingly, the title sufficing for nearly a century. Then, with the stroke of a bureaucrat's pen, Castle was changed to Eisenhower to commemorate the post war visit of American President Dwight Eisenhower. In 1983, though, as a result of public pressure, the original name was rightfully restored. The isolated pinnacle at the south-east end is now known as Eisenhower Tower, while the cairn and register are on a higher point slightly north-west of the Tower. The highest point actually lies some 3 km north-west at 720863 but is seldom visited. Try this outing from July on.

Drive to Castle Junction 31 km west of Banff via either the Trans-Canada Highway or the Bow Valley Parkway (Highway 1-A). The trailhead for Rockbound Lake is located on the north side of Bow Valley Parkway, 300 m east of Castle Junction Service Station, and across from the Youth Hostel by the Warden's residence. Park here.

From the parking area, follow the hiking trail for 8.4 km to Rockbound Lake, passing Tower Lake on the way. Rockbound Lake, enclosed by steep walls of dolomite and limestone, lies in the centre of the Castle Mountain Syncline, a product of geologically-significant Castle Mountain Thrust. The fault line is located slightly east, close to Helena Ridge. This transitional feature separates the older Main Ranges of the Rockies from the younger Front Ranges.

The dipping strata of Helena Ridge provides access to the first part of the route. Hike up the lower flanks on the east side of Rockbound Lake, passing through a gully in the rockband close to a large knoll at 746856. Although a

beaten path winds up and over this hump, you can also skirt along the exposed foot of it. Circle the lake counterclockwise across a broad, grassy terrace above the cliff band. This spacious ledge with its trickles of melt-water sits on limestone formed during the Middle Cambrian period, 530 million years ago.

Where the grassy terrace peters out, a short scramble up a gully leads to the upper bench which slopes gently towards numerous high points crowning the 4 km-long Castle Mountain massif. As you plod to the summit register, chasms along the crest reveal glimpses of the Bow Valley framed by buttresses of ancient Eldon limestone. This is the same rock formation comprising the near vertical face of Mount Yamnuska, another climbers mecca at the eastern edge of the Rockies.

From the top there are splendid views along Bow Valley with the summits of the Lake Louise group dominating the skyline.

If you are so inclined it is possible to **traverse** the entire mass of Castle Mountain end-to-end in a long day. Because it is difficult to descend at the north-west end, you are advised to head north-east from the highest point at 720863 towards Stuart Knob and descend scree slopes back to the terrace above Rockbound Lake. You could also traverse further around to include Helena Ridge. This all-inclusive excursion is recommended for those with boundless energy and enthusiasm for trudging.

Photo: Don Beers

The last section of Castle Mtn. route seen from Helena Ridge -– just a walk. H highest point

Stuart Knob Option 2850 m

Stuart Knob is the pointy little peak flanked by terrific talus slopes behind Castle Mountain, and is readily apparent from Trans-Canada Highway west of Banff. Lying 1.5 km north-west of Rockbound Lake, it is easily ascended by rubble slopes beyond the grassy terrace above the lake and knoll at 746856. Wander around left to the opposite side and scramble to the top which is actually higher than Castle Mountain. Who would have guessed?

Helena Ridge Option 2862 m

For scramblers wanting a better view but not quite up to the lengthy tramp up Castle Mountain, there is little difficulty in attaining the highest summit of Helena Ridge. This 5 km-long ridge lies north and east of Rockbound Lake, and is a wee bit higher than Castle. Try from July on.

From Rockbound Lake a wide gully gives access to the top at 745865 via gentle south-east slopes. Only moderate challenges are involved in continuing to a neighbouring vantage point only 1 km to the east and 75 m lower. Views include Bonnet Peak directly north and Mount Ball to the south. From either position you get a fuller appreciation of the considerable mass of Castle Mountain without the effort of actually walking it.

Although scree on this ascent is the tedious ski-pole type, keep in mind this is not just any old scree. This is 530 million year old scree. What caused it? A geologist might say that a movement known as the Castle Mountain Thrust is at fault.

Looking back from Castle Mtn. summit at ascent route from Rockbound Lake.
S Stuart Knob, H Helena Ridge

Television Peak Option 2970 m

TV Peak is the unnamed point much further along the Castle Mountain massif at 708893. It can be reached in 1 - 1.5 hours of easy plodding from Stuart Knob.

For those who care about such matters, this unnamed peak lying north-west of Castle Mountain eclipses both Stuart Knob and Helena Ridge in elevation. From Stuart Knob, the ascent is merely a long and unexciting plod as you continue north to circle the intervening bowl (718895), then gain a gentle ridge extending north-east from TV peak. Views from the top are respectable, but the walk is long.

Confident scramblers wishing an **alternate return** can descend the south-west side of TV Peak below the repeater building to gain the highway. Downclimbing a short, steep wall right near the top constitutes the crux. Note the rock's resemblance to stacks of shingles. This is not the only similarity — it is piled a bit precariously too. Continue west down easy terrain to tree-line and eventually, Bow Valley Parkway. Yet another plod ensues as you head for your vehicle, 9 km down the road near Castle Junction. By this time the whole business of peak-bagging will have begun to take on an air of pointlessness. Inquisitive stares by occupants of the many vehicles passing by adds to the lark.

Photo: Kris Thorsteinsson

TV Peak from Castle Mtn. — a long walk. Route circles to right and ascends right skyline ridge.
D Optional descent to 1-A Highway.

MOUNT WHYMPER 2845 m

Difficulty Moderate scrambling
via south slopes
Ascent time 2.5-4 hours
Height gain 1250 m
Map 82 N/1 Mount Goodsir

A fine viewpoint for the icy north face of neighbouring Mount Stanley, Mount Whymper plays host to visitors only occasionally. The beginning is a bit bushy. Higher up, early season visitors would benefit from the use of an ice-axe. Try from June on.

From Castle Junction on the Trans-Canada Highway, follow Kootenay Parkway (Highway 93) to Stanley Glacier parking lot, 3.4 km south of the Continental Divide.

There is room for considerable route variation on the ascent of Mount Whymper, but to minimize deadfall-bashing aim for avalanche slopes on the east side of the peak directly above the parking lot. When cliff-bands pose a problem, traverse left onto a more southerly aspect and continue up gullies and scree to the summit ridge. In June these gullies make for a terrific glissade, assuming you've brought an ice-axe for self-arrest should the event progress quicker than expected. Besides leap-frogging over burned timber which came down in a lightning-caused forest fire back in 1968, no real problems exist on the ascent. Remarkably, in spite of twenty-odd years of scouring by harsh climate, a casual brush against the charred snags instantly blackens the unwary's expensive outdoor gear, even today. That may be the most remarkable fact of the entire ascent.

For internationally-renowned climber, Englishman Edward Whymper, a first ascent of this minor peak in 1901 must have seemed trivial compared to his controversial conquest of the renowned Swiss Matterhorn some thirty years earlier. His love of the bottle may have limited his abilities. Despite employing four top-notch Swiss guides, his mountaineering accomplishments in the Rockies were relatively lackluster. Rather than recommend effective ways to bolster tourism potential of the Rockies, he chose to spend much of his time criticizing the hospitality of his host, Canadian Pacific Railway.

The south slopes.

STORM MOUNTAIN 3161 m

Difficulty A moderate scramble
via west slopes
Ascent time 3.5-6 hours
Height gain 1500 m
Map 82 N/1 Mount Goodsir

Storm Mountain is a brooding summit overlooking Castle Mountain Junction and Twin Lakes. It is frequently ascended via the sweeping north-east ridge by mountaineers who reserve the west side primarily for descent. Early in the summer though, when firm snow covers much tedious scree and vegetation in the old Vermilion Burn, this normal descent route constitutes an acceptable scramble. Try from June on.

From Castle Junction on the Trans-Canada Highway, drive 10 km south-west on the Kootenay Parkway (Highway 93). Park on the east side of the road 0.7 km south of the Continental Divide parking lot.

From the parking spot alongside the highway, cross the stream and head through burnt forest straight for the small valley on the west side of the peak (675738). The going becomes easier once you reach this valley. As you cross the boulder field you may marvel at one house-sized specimen of quartzite. Its ability to have withstood what must have been a substantial fall from adjacent cliffs says much for the quality of the rock.

Continue east towards scree slopes at the east end of the valley. These slopes are laborious and infinitely longer than expected, a good reason to go during June when you can make use of snow patches and an ice-axe. Upward progress reveals a quiet cirque to the north, complete with two alpine tarns characteristically rimmed by Lyall's larch. Towards the top of the slope short cliffs can be avoided by detouring left. Quickly the angle eases. As you trudge to the cairn, be sure to give the cornice on the summit ridge to the left a wide berth.

The north face of nearby Mount Ball, resplendent under its icy cap, rivets the gaze, while to the west stand Deltaform, Hungabee and the Goodsirs, all more than 3353 m high. On **descent** you may decide to detour over to the nearby tarns to while away any extra time. Otherwise, return the same way.

Storm Mountain was an accepted qualifying climb for new members at the Alpine Club of Canada's Vermilion Pass Camp in 1912. As one participant noted, "Those yielding slopes of splintered rock were a tiresome treadmill, but the climb seemed more worth the effort when the summit was reached....and the scenery at last began to present elements of beauty." The name is, of course, weather-related.

West slopes of Storm Mtn from Mt. Whymper.

MOUNT BALL 3311 m

Difficulty Moderate scrambling;
remote with bushwhacking
Ascent time 7-10 hours
Height gain 1820 m
Map 82 N/1 Mount Goodsir

Mount Ball is a dominant Rockies peak that can be seen from countless other peaks. Summit views are excellent and the trip suggests a feeling of remoteness throughout, but the approach is long. Few people who have ever reached Mount Ball by this route would want to repeat the ordeal. While the actual ascent is not difficult, it is the tedious flail through tracts

of forest, at times on sidehills, together with no trail or view that combine to sap the desire. Not until hours after starting do you escape the confines of Haffner Creek and experience pleasant going in the upper valley. Still, Mount Ball is a prominent peak and this is the least-technical and most direct way of reaching it. This fact, together with the knowledge that Beatrice Peak (3125 m, 681681) can be combined with marginally more effort should guarantee that at least a few hardy souls will take up the challenge. Besides, the bush is only tedious — not ferocious. Try from mid-July on.

From Castle Junction on the Trans-Canada Highway, follow Kootenay Parkway (Highway 93) to Marble Canyon campground, 7 km south of the Continental Divide.

Begin from the south-east corner of the campground by the creek. For the first half-hour a path above canyon walls on

the north side seduces you onward, only to deteriorate into thickets of bush and sidehill bashing. Continue as best you can, never out of earshot of the creek, for about two to three hours at which point you begin to reach the upper valley (665665). A cliffband jutting across the middle of the valley is circumvented on the right-hand side. Shortly after, open

Approaching Mt. Ball from Haffner Creek. Route enters cirque to left. B Beatrice Peak. S summit of Mt. Ball.

Photo: Kris Thorsteinsson

On Beatrice Peak. Route to Mt. Ball goes to left of intervening ridge, then up snow slopes.

larch meadows offer a welcome respite from the toil and a chance to study the squat shape of the objective. Finally, the trip shows signs of merit.

Though guarded by a horizontal belt of deteriorating cliffs, from this aspect, the snowy dome of Mount Ball appears tranquil. A cascading remnant of ice beyond lengthy lateral moraines hints of a once sizeable glacier having filled the valley. Early editions of the map still indicate this. The intended route of ascent soon diverges from this moraine, crossing karst pavement into a scree-filled cirque on the left between Beatrice and Ball (675678). The goal is to gain the ridge connecting the two. Numerous gullies cleave the rockband above scree slopes; on descent we found a particularly easy one directly below Mount Beatrice. From the ridge

between the two peaks an undulating plod, partly on snow, passes a rocky buttress on the left before rising gently to the top of Mount Ball.

Because the peak is recognizable from so many other summits, it seems logical that it would be a strategic viewpoint. It does not disappoint, although the reality of the long trek out will probably curtail the summit visit. With a round-trip time likely exceeding 14 hours, a head lamp and an early start are strongly recommended. An ice-axe should be carried.

Irish-born John Ball was a famed British alpinist and public servant who aided the Palliser Expedition through his position as Under-Secretary of State for the Colonies. Beatrice Schultz of the Alpine Club of Canada made her graduating climb on the peak bearing her name.

LAKE LOUISE

Mount Niblock	2976 m	moderate	p. 143
Mount Whyte	2983 m	difficult	p. 144
Mount Temple	3543 m	moderate	p. 146
Mount Fairview	2744 m	easy	p. 149
Eiffel Peak	3084 m	moderate	p. 150
Mount Bell	2910 m	moderate	p. 152

If Banff Park is a gallery of mountain landscapes, then Lake Louise must surely be the Master's corner. It was this gem that was so frequently flaunted on Canadian Pacific Railway's promotional literature around the turn of the century. The motive? To lure rich Europeans to the vast, unexplored region known as The Canadian Rockies. "Fifty Switzerlands in one", boasted one poster. More subtle advertising today includes the Canadian $20 bill which shows nearby Moraine Lake. This is merely a sample though. Everywhere at Lake Louise the view is dominated by high, craggy summits flanked by glistening glaciers and permanent snowfields.

While most of the larger peaks are not conducive to unroped scrambling — partly due to the need to cross these glaciers — there are still some good scrambles. Because the scenery ranks with the best in the Rockies, you should not visit this region expecting solitude. It's possibly the busiest part of Banff Park, and the peaks reflect this popularity. Mount Temple, highest in the area, often plays host to a half-dozen scramblers even on a day of "iffy" weather. By contrast, mountain tops in the Skoki locality are much less travelled, despite an abundance of backpackers and horse riders wandering the valleys.

Scrambles around Lake Louise may have a little different feel to them than ascents farther east. An ice-axe should be considered standard equipment for higher peaks, while routes frequently resemble mountaineering rather than "pure" scrambling — if there is such a thing! Strata in the surrounding peaks often lie horizontally, with weathering producing alternating bands of short steep cliffs and fairly flat ledges. You may find this a pleasant departure from tilted Front Range strata around Canmore and Kananaskis. The scree, however, shows no improvement. Quartzite is an important constituent of the Rockies' make-up here. When wet, this type of rock is much slicker than limestone as you may discover.

Due to the position along the Continental Divide, precipitation is heavier than in the Front Ranges. When the weather turns damp, snow may fall at any time of year and you can waste valuable vacation time waiting for an improvement. A short drive east to Canmore or Banff often escapes these inclement weather patterns.

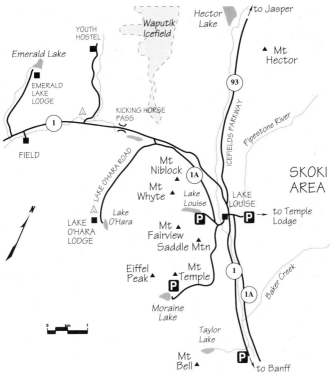

Access The Trans-Canada Highway provides access to the village of Lake Louise. To the east, the nearest town is Banff, while to the west, the first stop of any size is Golden, B.C. For those people without a car, Greyhound buses stop in on daily runs from both directions, and Brewster runs a daily shuttle from Calgary International Airport. Within the village, a well-signed road leads 5.5 km to Chateau Lake Louise. Some 4 km along, Moraine Lake Road diverges left and travels 12 km to the Valley of the Ten Peaks. Also diverging from the access road to Lake Louise is Highway 1A which offers an alternate route to and from Kicking Horse Pass on the Trans-Canada Highway.

Facilities One crowded, expensive shop used to be the sole source of supplies in the village, but since the advent of Samson Mall, shopping has taken a leap forward. Consumers now have the convenience of a Government liquor outlet, a laundromat with showers, a well-stocked grocery, a sports store, book store, and Laggan's bakery. Laggan's offers possibly the best dollar value of any eatery you'll ever find. Since opening, it has firmly established itself as a "must do" while in Lake Louise. Of the two gas stations in town, neither is open 24 hrs. Wilson Mountain Sports in Samson Mall (522-3636) rents equipment including bikes and ice-axes.

Lake Louise

Photo: Tony Daffern

Admiring the view of Mt Victoria from the summit of Mt Fairview

Accommodation Within the village are a campground and various hotels. Aside from camping, the Canadian Alpine Centre, jointly run by the Alpine Club of Canada and the Southern Alberta Hostelling Association, is probably the most affordable place to stay. Facilities available include a cafeteria, meeting rooms, cooking areas, sleeping and family rooms and a lounge. Reservations are accepted. Hotels in town are not for the budget-minded!

Two popular backcountry teahouses gratify the hiking crowd. Lake Agnes Teahouse is located on the approach to Mounts Niblock and Whyte, while Plain of Six Glaciers Teahouse lies below Mount Victoria, not far from the Mount Whyte descent route. Remember to take your hard currency — bartering will get you nowhere!

Information For information on trails, weather, backcountry regulations and permits, head to Parks Canada Information Centre at Samson Mall.

Wardens Should you be needing more concise information on current mountain conditions, it is sometimes possible to speak with one of the climbing wardens at their office in the Government building at the west end of Village Road. They would be glad to help you stay out of trouble. Normal hours are 0800-1630.

MOUNT NIBLOCK 2976 m

Difficulty Moderate scrambling
via Lake Agnes
Ascent time 3-6 hours
Height gain 1250 m
Map 82 N/8 Lake Louise

Mount Niblock is an increasingly popular Lake Louise scramble approached by a busy trail. Nearby Mount Whyte can also be included, allowing a different descent route to Plain of Six Glaciers Teahouse. Somewhat minor elevations compared to the surrounding giants of Lefroy, Victoria and Temple, these two lesser peaks have always been overlooked in favour of their loftier neighbours. They do, however, merit attention.

Attempting these peaks too early in the season is not advisable, particularly Mount Whyte and the optional south slope descent which could be too snowy and prone to wet snow avalanches. Most of June could be regarded as rushing it in a typical year. For these ascents, carry an ice-axe and know how to use it as you may be able to glissade some of the return trip. Crampons could also be considered, but are not usually necessary. During summer any snow on these routes normally softens considerably by mid-day. When visible, this hardware is sure to induce conversation among curious hordes which prowl the pathways. Be prepared to pose for pictures in high-season.

From Lake Louise townsite, follow the access road to Lake Louise. Turn left 100 m before the Chateau and park in the paved parking lot.

Wander along the paved lakeshore path past the Chateau to the signed Lake Agnes trail which forks right. Follow it for 3.4 km to Lake Agnes. Lake Agnes Teahouse will be closed if you've got off to a proper alpine start, so continue along the right-hand shore. Head towards scree slopes and cliffs under the high col connecting Niblock and Whyte.

Although you will be unlikely to see them early in the morning, tiny, furry "rock-rabbits" or Pika are occasionally glimpsed as they dart among the rocks. The boulders are prime spots for drying carefully harvested leaves and grasses which they collect for their winter hay-pile.

The easiest line from below the Niblock/Whyte col ascends talus on the right side rather than short cliffbands lying to the left. You may stumble onto

scratches of trail in places. If you do opt for the more challenging cliffbands, it is worth studying them on the approach since a multitude of potential routes cleave this Cambrian-aged belt. Although the rock is generally sound, eons of erosion have left rubble perched on ledges and filling gullies. You may have to dig for the solid stuff! Depending on the month, in early morning there could well be hard snow covering some scree. With an ice-axe and knowledge of its use, step-kicking reduces the grind.

On an early June ascent of late, an experienced party descended via a narrow snow gully which at that time of the season had a flowing meltwater stream hidden beneath soft snow. A snowbridge, probably weakened by combined actions of daytime heating and splashing water, collapsed, resulting in one person falling into a moat between a short cliff and surrounding snow. Her partner was unsuccessful in extricating her with fatal results. Scramblers would, therefore, be wise to con-

View from Lake Agnes of Mts. Niblock (right) and Whyte (left), with Niblock/Whyte col at centre.

sider this example and take care in selecting their route and time of ascent. If in doubt, wait it out — till July, if necessary. By then, much snow should have melted.

Once you reach the col and catch your breath, walk towards the buttress of Mount Niblock. Pretty weird rock here — black, blobby stuff that almost looks like it may have been molten at one time. It wasn't though. The only known occurrence of igneous rock anywhere in Banff Park occurs just south of Bow Lake. The rounded shape here must be due to weathering.

You can ascend either side of the buttress. The shadier left side may harbour snow, but otherwise offers no difficulties. Allow another 25 minutes to the top. Mount Niblock is one of the more favoured scrambles in the vicinity, and over the course of three recent summers some sixty parties have signed the register.

Mount Whyte Option

Mount Whyte is much more demanding than Niblock, requiring better scrambling and route-finding abilities, a head for heights as well as familiarity with the use of an ice-axe. Allow about 35 minutes from Niblock/Whyte col.

Proceed towards Mount Whyte from the Niblock/Whyte col. When the ridge narrows you may be forced to make a brief detour right before it begins to steepen. At this point traverse left for some 40 m on a prominent scree ledge towards a right-slanting gully. This gully may be icy and wet, and without crampons would be a quick ticket down over high cliffs. Avoid it. Ledges along the right-hand side of the gully are a safer bet but demand respect even when dry, since your position is fairly exposed. After surmounting this crux section, traverse along the foot of a rockwall.

Watch for a likely-looking spot to scramble up firm ledges of Eldon limestone to the summit ridge. The cairn lies a short distance beyond.

Here you are surrounded by some of the finest examples of mountain majesty in the entire Canadian Rockies. From the summit, the dazzling Upper Victoria Glacier is complemented by Mount Lefroy and the ancient tongue of glacier snaking from Abbott Pass to the Death Trap below. Abbott Pass Hut is barely visible — a minuscule dot straddling the pass between stalwart guardians of stone. Constructed only partially of rock quarried from the immediate vicinity, this shelter demanded some two tons of materials be packed by horse as far up the ice as possible. Swiss guides then man-handled these same materials through the deeply-crevassed upper glacier to the hut site. With its roof-top diverting drizzle into both Alberta and British Columbia since 1922, the shelter stands in simple, silent testimony to the unwavering persistence of those pioneers of the peaks. Until recently, it held the unique distinction of being the highest refuge in the Canadian Rockies at 2922 m, but has since relinquished the title to the Colgan Hut above Moraine Lake.

On your **return**, rather than retrace the ascent route, a simpler option is to scramble down a short distance on the south side of Mount Whyte towards its south-west outlier. You can then descend lengthy scree/snow slopes which lead to Plain of Six Glaciers hiking trail. This descent has the added advantage of placing you handy to the red-roofed teahouse where home-baked pie and goodies can be appreciated. (Did you bring any money?)

In 1886 two Canadian Pacific Railway officials intent on fishing the icy waters of "Lake of the Little Fishes" visited the jewel of the Rockies — Lake Louise. Their catch has gone unrecorded but Mounts Niblock and Whyte today bear their names, a custom adopted by none-too-modest railway dignitaries of the day.

Mt. Whyte from Mt. Niblock. W summit of Mt. Whyte, NW Niblock/Whyte col. SW outlier to right.

145

MOUNT TEMPLE 3543 m

Difficulty A moderate scramble via
south-west ridge and face on scree/
snow slopes
Ascent time 3.5-6 hours
Height gain 1690 m
Map 82 N/8 Lake Louise

Mount Temple is the ultimate scramble.
Towering majestically over the Lake Louise
environs this hulking giant, third highest in
the southern Rockies, presents an impreg-
nable palisade of vertical rock capped by
perpetual snow and ice. This impression is
a facade. Tucked away on the south-west
side, cunningly hidden from any road, lies a
straightforward and much-frequented "tourist" route. Consequently, Temple is the most
accessible peak over 11,000' (3353 m) in
the entire Canadian Rockies chain, and
likely the most often climbed.

Since 1894, when three intrepid members
of the Yale-Lake Louise Club clambered
up this face, hundreds of adventurers
have wheezed their way to the snowy
summit. It should not, however, be treated
lightly. In 1955 seven young teen-aged
boys, poorly equipped and inexperienced, perished here in Canada's worst-
ever mountaineering accident. Ironically,
adults supervising the group attempted to
hold Parks Canada liable in the aftermath,
citing their own ignorance a result of inad-
equate information from Parks personnel.
Therefore, anyone in doubt of conditions,
(either their own or that of the mountain!)
is advised to consult the Lake Louise
Warden Office before heading out. In a
typical year, the route is in condition by
mid-July. An ice-axe is recommended

From Lake Louise townsite, drive 15 km
to Moraine Lake parking lot.

Hike along the shore of Moraine Lake to
where Larch Valley trail begins just
past the newly constructed lodge. Relentless switchbacks lead past a junction (keep right) into the flat, open
meadows of Larch Valley. Continue up
further switchbacks to Sentinel Pass.
The final approach affords a clear, albeit foreshortened view of the route,
and there should be no difficulties finding a trail beaten into scree at the start
of the south-west ridge.

Churn your way up the scree. Below
the first towering wall, traverse horizontally right on a path dotted with
cairns and ascend the third gully to the
right to overcome the black rockband.
The first two gullies are much more

demanding. Continue up more gravel-
strewn black ledges, angling right to
reach an easy spot to scramble up the
next rockband, which this time is grey.
Cairns are abundant and seem to multi-
ply yearly. Although the rock is generally firm, expect the customary rubble
on ledges and slabs — caution needed.
Well-trodden paths entice you up the
slope to a final band of firm, cream-
coloured rock. Handholds are plentiful
and ascending this short obstacle will
pose no challenge.

On regaining the south-west ridge,
you leave all technical difficulties behind, but the terrain is still steep and
the rubble precarious. Even without
snow an ice-axe helps immensely. As
you heave upward through the ever-
thinning air, myriads of channels worn
in the scree indicate the crowds this

Photo: Tony Daffern   *Temple's "tourist" route seen from Larch Valley. S Sentinel Pass.*

From the top of Mt. Temple, the nearby Ten Peaks grace the skyline. Goodsir Towers at far right..

Ascending a rockband.

The view as you might expect is superb. On a clear day the stark, granitic spires of the Bugaboos are visible 80 km to the west. During late September, golden larches, a dusting of snow and the characteristic smoke-free fall horizon render this panorama particularly satisfying.

Although the ascent is a simple undertaking in dry conditions, Mount Temple is a major peak and should be treated as such. Sufficient extra clothing and an ice-axe are strongly suggested. At the time of the first ascent in 1894, scholar-cum-mountaineer Walter Wilcox surmised that given the known temperature at Lake Louise and that which he recorded on top, it was safe to say it never exceeded 40 degrees Fahrenheit on the summit. Prepare accordingly.

route draws. The angle relents for the final plod to the summit cairn, allowing you some respite at last. Be wary of cornices on your right which project over the east face.

Sir Richard Temple, for whom the mountain was named, was president of the Economic Science and Statistics Section, British Association, 1884.

MOUNT FAIRVIEW 2744 m

Difficulty Easy hike via Saddleback
Ascent time 2-4 hours
Height gain 1000 m
Map 82 N/8 Lake Louise

Mount Fairview gives a terrific aerial view of Mount Victoria, Victoria Glacier, the north face of Mount Temple and the Bow Valley. The outing is an interesting addition to a favoured Lake Louise vicinity hike. With very little extra effort minuscule Saddle Mountain (2434m) can be ascended at the same time. If while in Lake Louise your time and energy are limited, this trip probably makes the best use of those precious resources. Try from mid-June on.

From Lake Louise townsite, follow the access road to Chateau Lake Louise. Turn left 100 m before the Chateau and park in the paved parking lot.

Begin near the boathouse on the lake shore and follow the signed path 3.7 km to Saddleback. Charred remains of the resthouse that once catered to turn-of-the-century trekkers are still evident more than fifty years after cancellation of its lease in 1937. From among scattered Lyall's larches at the pass a discernible trail zigzags up scree to the summit, offering no difficulty. Although not as lofty as nearby peaks, Fairview is aptly named as stunning summit vistas will undoubtedly prove, assuming the weather co-operates.

Photo: Gillean Daffern

From Saddle Mtn. a view of the ascent route from Saddleback.

EIFFEL PEAK 3084 m

Difficulty Moderate scrambling
via south-east slopes
Ascent time 2.5-4.5 hours
Height gain 1230 m
Map 82 N/8 Lake Louise

Eiffel Peak overlooks a most famous scene in the Canadian Rockies — the Valley of the Ten Peaks. The surrounding landscape is no less dazzling. Hordes of visitors frequent the area, particularly during fall when larches display coats of golden splendour. Crowds such as these may be just the impetus needed to send you scurrying up Eiffel Peak, a convenient lofty avenue of escape. On days of unsettled weather the excursion is a practical alternative to more demanding Mount Temple, and grants you a good view of Temple's normal route. Although there may be bigger peaks nearby, Eiffel's location in the midst of all this grandeur makes the ascent a natural attraction which should be on any scrambler's list. Try from July on.

From Lake Louise townsite, drive 15 km to Moraine Lake parking lot.

Hike along the shore of Moraine Lake to where Larch Valley trail begins just past the newly constructed lodge. Relentless switchbacks lead to the flat, open meadows of Larch Valley where three peaks command the scene. Mounts Temple and Pinnacle form the stalwart buttresses of Sentinel Pass while to the left, a sweeping ridge rises to the upper-most heights of Eiffel Peak.

Wander south across a small stream and gain the broad shoulder arcing gracefully skyward towards Eiffel's summit 850 m above. Numerous trails in the scree attest to the popularity of the objective. To put difficulties into perspective, a past summit register entry recorded a successful canine ascent. Near the top, wide gullies lead through the rockband whereupon short, rubbly slabs give way to the summit and cairn.

On the north-west side stands an imposing 70 m-high pillar called Eiffel Tower, and it is for this feature that the peak is named. First climbed in 1952, this exacting ascent required nine hours from the separating notch despite the small vertical gain involved. It has been largely ignored since then.

Normal route begins at Larch Valley and is not as steep as this suggests. R rockbands.

Studying Eiffel Tower from the summit.

MOUNT BELL 2910 m

Difficulty A moderate scramble
via south-west slopes
Ascent time 4.5-7 hours
Height gain 1500 m
Map 82 N/8 Lake Louise

Mount Bell is a strategic viewpoint overlooking Taylor, Boom and O'Brien Lakes. Although the approach is fairly long, it is pleasant, visiting no less than

four secluded alpine tarns en route. Above tree-line, views include the seldom-glimpsed Boom Glacier area, as well as The Rockwall in Kootenay Park and further west, the Bugaboos of the Purcell Range. Depending on snow conditions, part of the descent can provide an exhilarating glissade. An ice-axe is recommended for this route; try it from mid-June on.

Drive to Taylor Lake trailhead located at a gravel pull-off area on the south side of the Trans-Canada Highway, 8.1 km west of Castle Junction.

From the parking lot, cross the creek and follow the well-graded hiking trail 8.4 km to Taylor Lake. This clear body of water is an agreeable place to halt, and you may have trouble tearing yourself away from the picnic tables conveniently located nearby. Brooding walls of Mount Bell shadow the lake and

reveal no easy line of ascent from this aspect, a situation not uncommon to north faces of peaks in the Rockies. The trail continues along the south side of the outlet stream and in 2 km reaches O'Brien Lake. Follow along the right-hand shore through stands of Lyall's Larch and across carpets of wildflowers to the waterfall at the west end of the lake. Although there is no marked trail, grovel up the hillside to a beautiful valley hosting two diminutive meltwater ponds.

As you continue past these ponds over much broken rock and debris, note the obvious col at the far end of the valley. This notch gives access to the easy-angled south slopes of Mount Bell. Because the wide, 150 m-high gully leading up to the col faces north, the snow may possibly be frozen in the morning. An ice-axe is therefore recommended for early season ascents, and crampons could also be considered. This slope grants a superb glissade when the snow softens a little and will likely be a highlight of the trip. After ascending this incline to the col, a grand scene bursts forth, begging a stop. Range upon range rear up in an infinite array of shapes as backdrop to the surrealistic blues of Boom Lake.

Work around to the south and south-west up scree and eroded sandstone towards huge lichen-covered quartzite blocks. Short chimneys cleaving firm rock will provide entertainment. Easier terrain followed by pinnacles along the south-west ridge leads towards the summit. Walk around these on the left-hand side. The final section requires a detour to the right, going below a large block which initially appears to be perched directly across the route.

Mount Bell is named for Dr. Frederick Bell, founding member of the ACC, and his sister Miss Nora Bell, also an Alpine Club member. Coincidentally, she accompanied the first ascent party of 1959.

Boom Lake Approach

An optional approach is available from Boom Lake. The total distance of this alternative may be shorter and it should not require ice-axe or crampons, but it is bushy and lacks a trail for much of the way.

Begin 7 km west of Castle Junction on the Kootenay Parkway (Highway 93) at a paved parking area. Follow Boom Lake trail to the lake, then thrash along the right-hand shore to any open gully or slope which will allow you to reach the ridge above. Going west along the ridge crest is straightforward once you reach it. Continue to the col and the south side of Mount Bell as for the O'Brien Lake approach. The two routes meet at this point.

Opposite: Final stretch of the SW ridge.

South side of Mt Bell from above Boom Lake. C col where two routes join.

SKOKI AREA

Ptarmigan Peak	3059 m	moderate	p. 156
Mount Richardson	3086 m	easy	p. 157
Pika Peak	3033 m	difficult	p. 158
Skoki Mountain	2697 m	easy	p. 159
Fossil Mountain	2946 m	easy	p. 160
Oyster Peak	2777 m	moderate	p. 161
Mount Redoubt	2902 m	moderate	p. 162
Brachiopod Mountain	2650 m	easy	p. 163
Anthozoan Mountain	2695 m	easy	p. 163

The Skoki area of Lake Louise is a true paradise for scramblers. Few locations in the Rockies can provide as many enjoyable ascents in such a spectacular alpine location — and altogether free of bushwacking. You could conceivably camp for a week and climb a new peak each day. Generally, the overall quality of the rock tends to be better than many Rockies scrambles. Perhaps the only negative aspect is the unavoidable trudge (or bike) up some 4 km of Temple Lodge Road to the trailhead. However, the walk-in does pay dividends. As one turn-of-the-century visitor noted, "Looking back the view of Mount Temple, Paradise Valley and the Ten Peaks is a wonder, and you realize that in order to see these mountains you must really cross the Bow Valley and climb up on the other side."

In spite of heavy horse traffic and numerous visits by backpackers, Skoki Valley retains a distinctly wild nature. In past years, lodge staff have witnessed wolves passing through, and fishermen have glimpsed wolverine as well. On one especially unforgettable trip, after a young grizzly visited our camp one evening, we were enchanted by the rare sight of a sow grizzly with no less than four tiny cubs hurrying off in the soft light the following morning. Had I been alone, I would have probably have felt less enchanted. Upon being notified of these sightings, Park officials were quick to close the area temporarily for the longevity of all parties concerned.

Since heavy snowfall is the norm here, July to October is the preferred period for scrambling.

Backcountry camping permits must be obtained from the Parks Canada Information Centre in Lake Louise.

Access From the overpass at Lake Louise townsite on the Trans-Canada Highway, drive 1.6 km towards Lake Louise ski area. Turn right onto Temple Lodge access road and continue for 1 km to Fish Creek parking lot. Park here.

Hike or bike Temple Lodge access road for 4 km to Temple Lodge. Bikes are not allowed beyond this point. Pass the Avalanche Research Station and ascend the ski run 200 m to the start of the well-used trail. Hidden Lake campsite is located a few minutes walk north of Half-way Hut (closed to overnight visitors) some 4 km from Temple Lodge. To reach Baker Lake campground continue over Boulder Pass and along the north (left) shore of Ptarmigan Lake to the east end of Baker Lake. For Skoki Lodge and the backcountry turn left (north) from the east end of Ptarmigan Lake and climb over Deception Pass into Skoki Valley.

Accomodation For those people planning to spend time in this area, the backcountry campsite at Hidden Lake serves as an ideal base for ascents of Richardson, Pika, Ptarmigan, Fossil, Redoubt and Heather Ridge. Baker Lake campsite is better situated for doing Oyster, Anthozoan and Brachiopod peaks. Skoki Lodge, a rustic backcountry chalet beside Skoki Mountain, caters mainly to trail-riding parties in summer but will usually sell snacks to non-guests. Another backcountry campground is located 1 km north of the lodge.

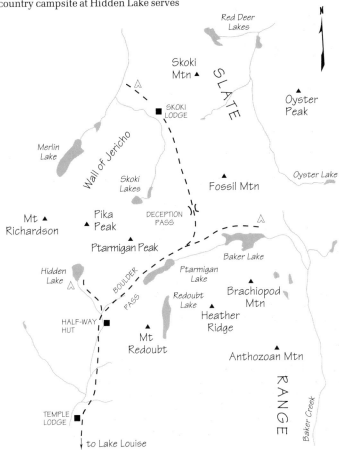

PTARMIGAN PEAK 3059 m

Difficulty Moderate scramble
via south scree slopes; exposure
Ascent time 2.5-5 hours
from Hidden Lake
Height gain 780 m
Map 82 N/8 Lake Louise

Ptarmigan Peak is a straightforward ascent that is feasible earlier in the season than its neighbours. It is sometimes climbed in winter. Near the top, a short, mildly exposed dip adds variety.

From Hidden Lake, gain the broad south slopes slightly west of Boulder Pass. Keeping more to the left of the wide rubble incline allows pleasant scrambling rather than plain old scree plodding. Just before the highest point at the east end, the ridge dips and narrows for 5 m directly above a long narrow gully cleaving the south side. To this point the way is easy and the problems few. This brief section is only of moderate challenge but does interrupt the simplicity of the ascent momentarily. Crossing this arête exposes you to a magnificent drop on the north side.

Occasionally, when avalanche conditions are favourable, ski parties ascend this peak, but judging by entries in the register, lads of the British Army mountain training units seem to have the greatest affinity for the mountain.

From the top, Mount Hector commands the northerly vista. When viewed from easterly and southerly directions such as when you drive west towards Lake Louise, many people have noticed an apparent resemblance between Mount Hector's outline and the popular cartoon dog "Snoopy" in a familiar prone position atop his dog house.

View from Redoubt: R Mt Richardson, P Pika Peak, Pt Ptarmigan Peak, H Hidden Lake.

MOUNT RICHARDSON 3086 m

Difficulty Easy scramble
via scree on south aspect;
Moderate via Richardson/Pika col
Ascent time 2-4 hours from Hidden
Lake
Height gain 800 m
Map 82 N/8 Lake Louise

Mount Richardson is the highest peak in the Skoki area, and provides an enjoyable scramble with an option to traverse and descend a different way. When camping at Hidden Lake the mountain is on your doorstep. Map editions as late as 1980 erroneously indicate massive glaciation covering most of the peak and extending east to Pika and Ptarmigan Peak, but this is not so. Try from July on.

An early morning jaunt up the south ridge of Mt Richardson. The Lake Louise group behind.

From Hidden Lake the south ridge offers a straightforward way to this expansive summit. Alternatively, you can easily reach the top after scrambling to the col between Richardson and Pika, though the slope above the col is often snowy and may require step-kicking and an ice-axe. This route also serves for descending and can be used to complete a traverse. Although the summit ridge isn't particularly narrow, be aware of cornices and glacier on the north side.

A **traverse** of Richardson lends itself well to a supplementary excursion over to the west ridge of Pika Peak — a worthwhile and recommended day trip from the campsite. Note that the ascent of the latter is rated "difficult" in comparison to the easy trudge up Richardson.

Sir John Richardson was Surgeon and Naturalist on the Franklin Arctic Expeditions.

PIKA PEAK 3033 m

Difficulty Difficult scrambling via
Richardson/Pika col and west ridge
Ascent time 2-4 hours from Hidden
Lake
Height gain 750 m
Map 82 N/8 Lake Louise

Though a grade or two more difficult
than nearby Richardson with which it is
often combined, Pika is a delightful
scramble once the snow has gone and
the rock is dry. As noted by mountaineers Delafield and Earle in 1911, "this
(westerly) arête, which at a distance
looks difficult, and which, in fact, is
steep, is composed of rocks so broken
as to render the ascent quite easy."

Gain the Richardson/Pika col via either the lower flanks of Pika above
Hidden Lake or by traversing from
nearby Richardson. The ridge to the
summit consists of several short steep
steps, sometimes cleft by chimneys
which facilitate the ascent. The rock is
excellent — firm and rough in texture.
Avoid straying too far around to the
exposed north side where it drops
abruptly to a pocket glacier below. Instead, stick fairly close to the crest.

Protruding like a stony fin just north
of Pika Peak is an impressive free-
standing wall of rock known as the
Wall of Jericho.

Although I don't recall seeing it, Pika
Peak is apparently named for a rock
formation near the top resembling a
mountain pika, or "rock rabbit".

The free-standing Wall of Jericho from Pika Peak.

SKOKI MOUNTAIN 2697 m

Difficulty An easy ascent
via north scree slopes
Ascent time 1-2 hours from Skoki
Lodge; 4-6 hours from Hidden Lake
Height gain 530 m from Skoki Lodge;
735 m from Hidden Lake
Map 82 N/9 Hector Lake

Skoki Mountain is a quick little ascent right beside Skoki Lodge. This diminutive mountain has been ascended by at least nine different routes by Edwin Knox, a former employee of historic Skoki Lodge. The most common way utilizes a wide swath, actually an ancient logging road, hacked into dense forest. Try from July on.

Maybe after tea... Skoki Mtn. is an easy ascent via the left-hand slopes. Route starts near Skoki Lodge.

The backcountry campsite 1 km north of Skoki Lodge makes the most sensible starting point for this outing. If you are camping at Hidden Lake, the approach will be much longer. During the 8 km approach, you must gain some 200 m elevation to cross Deception Pass, then promptly lose this amount and more before reaching Skoki Lodge and the base of the peak. The modest summit hardly justifies this long-winded march.

Begin immediately back of the lodge near the present site of the outhouse. After rising through forest, the path leads to open meadows at tree-line on the north side, whereupon a plod up open scree slopes completes the climb.

An early visitor to the region hailed from Skokie, Illinois. Also, Skoki is purported to be an Indian word meaning "marsh" or "swamp", some of which lies in areas to the east.

FOSSIL MOUNTAIN 2946 m

Difficulty An easy ascent
from Deception Pass
Ascent time 2-3 hours from Hidden
Lake
Height gain 670 m
Map 82 N/8 Lake Louise,

82 N/9 Hector Lake
Backcountry skiers frequently ascend this
peak en route to Skoki Lodge.

Fossil Mtn. rises above Ptarmigan Lake and Deception Pass.

From Deception Pass, tramp up the windblown west slope, usually bare even in the deep of winter. Coral fossils litter the route sparking interest in an otherwise mundane march, but to suggest the trek is pointless would be a fabrication. Viewing Skoki Lakes, cerulean jewels snugly nestled between Ptarmigan Peak and the Wall of Jericho, is in itself reward enough. After a group of American mountaineers saw them in 1911, they named the lower of the two Lakes Myosotis, "not only on account of its color, but also on account of its forget-me-not qualities."

On **descent** you can often glissade the broad south-west gully to Deception Pass if you have an ice-axe. Steer clear of this trough in winter — wind-loading can create soft slab avalanche conditions which resulted in two fatalities in the winter of 1988.

160

OYSTER PEAK 2777 m

Difficulty A moderate scramble via west-facing slopes
Ascent time 1.5-3 hours (south summit) from Baker Lake
Height gain 600 m
Map 82 N/9 Hector Lake

Oyster Peak affords good scrambling to the south summit and along the ridge to the north end. Views of Pipestone and Red Deer valleys are excellent.

From Baker Lake campsite, stroll across Baker Creek valley and ascend straightforward slopes at the south end. Continue unimpeded along the broad crest for an hour to the true summit at the north end which is 40 m higher, then return by descending in a westerly direction to Baker Creek valley. There is plenty of room for variation on both ascent and descent.

Photo: Don Beers

The tiny lake below the north end was at one time known as "Hatchet Lake", a name that has been lost to time since the ponds became collectively referred to as the Red Deer Lakes.

The discovery of large quantities of fossils similar to common oysters induced geologist G.M. Dawson to title this peak accordingly. It is likely they were brachiopods which you may also notice on your ascent.

It's a ridge! No, it's Oyster Peak. Route follows the ridge from right to left to the summit at S.

161

MOUNT REDOUBT 2902 m

Difficulty Moderate/difficult scrambling
via north-west ridge
Ascent time 2.5-5 hours from Hidden
Lake
Height gain 475 m (approximately) with
loss and regain
Map 82 N/8 Lake Louise

The north-west ridge of Mount Redoubt
gives good scrambling in grand surroundings. Try from mid-July on.

Mt. Redoubt showing route. R Redoubt Lake

From Hidden Lake head up over Boulder
Pass and along the south shore of Ptarmigan Lake. Follow a rather circuitous
route going south towards Redoubt
Lake, easily up over the north ridge of the
objective, then losing elevation to cross a
small rubble-strewn basin (not glaciated
as some maps show) en route to the
north-west ridge. This meandering line
isn't problematic — merely roundabout.
Once you actually attain the north-west
ridge the scrambling is delightful with
many horizontal ledges and big firm
handholds. The backdrop is a signature

of Lake Louise, displaying giants like
Victoria, Lefroy and Temple, three of the
fifty-three Rockies peaks exceeding
11,000' (3353 m). A final short cliff below the summit plateau is readily surmounted on the right.

A.O. Wheeler, founding member
and president of the Alpine Club of
Canada, fancied the mountain re-
sembled a military formation known
as a redoubt where forces are drawn up
in a tight cluster; often a last stand
attempt with no flanking defenses.

BRACHIOPOD MOUNTAIN 2650 m
ANTHOZOAN MOUNTAIN 2695 m

Difficulty Easy scrambles via westerly aspect
Ascent time 1.5-3 hours from Baker Lake
Height gain 410 m
Map 82 N/8 Lake Louise

Neither of these objectives poses any difficulty; each is readily ascended by west-facing scree slopes. With a camp at Baker Lake, both can be done in one day. Each of these peaks is a good argument for use of ski poles due to the looseness of the terrain. Try from July on.

From Baker Lake campsite ford the outlet stream to approach these peaks. If starting from Hidden Lake, either cross the meadows between Ptarmigan and Baker Lakes, or follow around the south shore of Ptarmigan Lake from Boulder Pass.

Clamber up the west slope of whichever one you have chosen. As a final respite from rubble, Brachiopod offers a brief change of regimen by way of a short slab immediately before topping out, whereas Anthozoan — more or less a continuation of the same ridge but far-

ther south — is entirely a slog. Nearby Heather Ridge to the west is an equally simple outing via west slopes.

Brachiopod is a common fossil found hereabouts; Anthozoan is a particular class of fossil. The Mount Brachiopod first ascent party in 1911 found "five species of coral, three varieties of Brachiopods, a sponge and several other fossils such as Crinoids, Bryozoa, etc." This proliferation of fossils is an intriguing aspect of the Southesk Formation — 370 million year old rock which comprises most of the west face.

Photo: Don Beers

B Brachiopod, A Anthozoan showing easy west slopes.

FIELD

Mount Bosworth	2771 m	difficult	p. 166
Mount Field	2635 m	easy	p. 167
Paget Peak	2560 m	easy	p. 168
Mount Burgess	2599 m	easy	p. 170
Mount Carnarvon	3040 m	difficult	p. 172
Mount Stephen	3199 m	difficult	p. 174
Narao Peak	2974 m	moderate	p. 176
Mount Yukness	2847 m	moderate	p. 179

Less touristy than Lake Louise is the placid community of Field, B.C. lying 25 km farther west on the Trans-Canada Highway. It is the administrative centre for 1300 sq km Yoho National Park which encompasses a rugged belt on the western slope of the Rockies where rushing streams begin their headlong journey to the Pacific. "Yoho" is said to be an exclamation of wonder in the Stoney tongue, and believably so. A tremendous amount of vertical relief separates summit and valley in this area west of the Continental Divide. Daunting amounts of elevation gain challenge scramblers on Mounts Stephen or Carnarvon — far above what most peaks demand. Like Lake Louise, snow accumulations here are heavy and even summer weather can be nasty, so the effective season is typically short. While Calgary and Kananaskis bask in a chinook during March or April, Field and Lake Louise are usually enduring a blizzard. It is these storms which spawn chinook conditions in areas farther east. Like ascents near Lake Louise, carry an ice-axe, at least on higher peaks. If you don't have one, visit Wilson's Sports in Lake Louise for rentals.

Access The Trans-Canada Highway accesses the town of Field which lies 35 minutes east of Golden and 20 minutes west of Lake Louise. Greyhound buses stop daily.

Facilities and Accommodation in Field includes campsites, hostels, bed & breakfasts as well as chalets and bungalows. Amiskwi Hostel is right in Field, while Whiskey Jack Hostel is located near the end of Yoho Valley Road which branches off the Trans-Canada Highway at the bottom of Field Hill. Kicking Horse Campground, Cathedral Mountain Chalets and a small store are found here too. At the end of the road is a walk-in campground by spectacular Takakkaw Falls. Farther west of Field are additional campgrounds. If you're not seeking budget accommodation, try West Louise Lodge at the top of Field Hill. They also carry some groceries. If price is of absolutely no concern, Emerald Lake Lodge offers luxuries like saunas and a hot tub. If the weather won't co-operate, try the exercise room on the premises! For shopping, the only store in Field is "The Siding" which offers meals, groceries and liquor.

If you plan on going to Lake O'Hara for Mount Yukness, once you've made the necessary bus reservations (Ph 604-343-6433), there is a choice of either the campground, Lake O'Hara Lodge, or an Alpine Club of Canada hut for overnight visitors. The Lodge is expensive and entertains its own exclusive clientele who book well ahead. The campground retains 10 of the 30 sites on a first-come first-served basis. Contact Parks Canada in Field (phone number as above) for reservations. The Alpine Club office in Canmore (Ph 678-5855) takes bookings for the Elizabeth Parker Hut. The hut is normally locked when no custodian is present.

Recently opened at Lake O'Hara is *Le Relais*, a small day facility selling soft drinks, tea, and snacks. This non-profit stand seems to be fulfilling its intended duty — the nearby O'Hara Lodge's front steps are no longer crowded at tea-time. Remember your cash if you go.

Information Almost any information concerning trails, permits, camping, lodging and a thousand other subjects is cheerily dispensed at the Park Information Centre (open at 8 a.m.). You'll find it across from the gas station at the turn-off into Field. To climb Mount Stephen, you will need to stop in here and obtain a special permit since you must pass the restricted Stephen Fossil beds area.

Wardens Yoho Park Warden Office is situated at Boulder Creek Compound, a few kilometres west of the town on the north side of the highway.

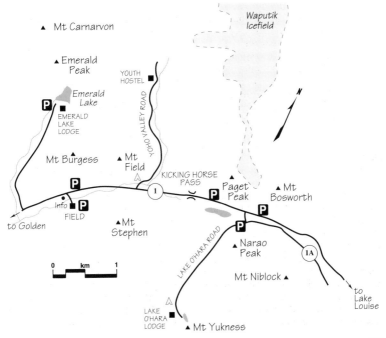

MOUNT BOSWORTH 2771 m

Difficulty Difficult scrambling for 30 m via south slopes and east ridge
Ascent time 2.5-4 hours
Height gain 1110 m
Map 82 N/8 Lake Louise

Mount Bosworth is a small, easily approached peak on the crest of the Continental Divide, boasting spectacular views of nearby major summits. The only real challenge occurs just before the top at a section of rubbly, black rock. An optional descent route allows a traverse. Anyone finding themselves in the area should consider a short outing up Mount Bosworth. The view of the peak as seen from the Trans-Canada Highway suffers from foreshortening. The route is more distinguishable from the 1-A highway and you may prefer to drive over there (intersection is 0.6 km west) for a look before starting. Try about late June or July.

Park on the shoulder of the Trans-Canada Highway at a huge avalanche slope, 0.6 km east of Highway 1-A intersection and 2.3 km west of Yoho National Park east boundary sign near Field.

Tramp straight up the avalanche slope — assuming the avalanche season is over of course! A minor rockband partway up

the slope is surmounted via a gully which may be damp but not likely to be flowing any significant amount. Cross over scree slopes (left) to a more westerly gully above tree-line, aiming to top out on the main ridge immediately east of the true summit which is visible at this point. Work slightly left of the ridge, crossing another gully below the final obstacle — 30 m of more difficult scrambling on ledges and up corners to overcome a belt of black strata. The cairn and register are 10 minutes further on.

If the weather co-operates you will be treated to a panorama which includes the icy north face of Mount Victoria to the south and the impressive bulk of the Goodsirs to the right. Ski-tourers may recognize familiar landmarks on the Wapta Icefields to the north such as the snowy face of Mount Collie.

As a **variation on descent**, scree slopes to the west lead to an intermittently flowing drainage and the Trans-Canada Highway. This route involves a fair amount of bushwacking and is definitely NOT worth considering as a route of ascent.

G. M. Bosworth was fourth Vice-President of the Canadian Pacific Railway.

Photo: Don Beers

A avalanche gully, C crux on east ridge.

MOUNT FIELD 2635 m

Difficulty An easy ascent
from Burgess Pass
Ascent time 2.5-4 hours
Height gain 1365 m
Map 82 N/8 Lake Louise

Mount Field is a very non-committing ascent offering a unique viewpoint for Mount Stephen's north glacier and distant Takakkaw Falls. One wonders why

this bump at the extremity of Mount Wapta's south-south-east extension has been designated a separate peak. The ascent of Mount Field is one of the simplest in the vicinity, as all but the final 400 vertical metres of elevation gain uses the well-graded Burgess Pass hiking trail. Views are worthwhile, but your accomplishment may not impress friends. Try from mid-June on.

Park at Burgess Pass trailhead on the north side of the Trans-Canada Highway, 0.4 km east of Field.

Follow Burgess Pass hiking trail, crossing the only source of water within 20 minutes. Continue to a signed junction at the top of the pass, gained after a stiff two hour walk. Take the Yoho Pass/Yoho Lake option to where it curves

Mt. Field forms the east buttress of Burgess Pass. W Mt Wapta.

left (north) towards Mount Wapta, and here leave the trail and trudge up shale and scree slopes. Trend right, aiming to intercept a dry gully which drains south. The simplest place to breach the short rock band is above this gully at the southern-most end.

Mount Stephen's north glacier is revealed in a much-expanded and more engaging view than the normal foreshortened glimpse from Field Hill. The distant pointy snow-peak left of Mount Wapta is Mount Des Poilus; further right are Yoho Glacier, Mount Balfour and Takakkaw Falls. Slightly north of you along the ridge towards Mount Wapta sits Walcott Quarry of the World-famous Burgess Fossil Beds. This site is a re-

stricted access area and unescorted visitors are NOT allowed. Spot checks for would-be fossil hunters are ongoing, and thieves are prosecuted. Take solace in knowing that you would find little of interest anyway — authorized "digs" occur periodically through summer months and these meticulous groups generally leave no stone unturned.

Cyrus West Field, promoter of the first Trans-Atlantic cable, visited this area at the insistence of CPR bigwig Cornelius Van Horne, who then patronizingly named it after his guest — the sole reason being to secure investment for continued railway construction. Though amused, Mr. Field didn't bite.

PAGET PEAK 2560 m

Difficulty An easy ascent via
Paget Lookout trail
Ascent time 1.5-3 hours
Height gain 1000 m
Map 82 N/8 Lake Louise

Paget Peak is a minor prominence situated high above Kicking Horse River on the western slopes of the Continental Divide. This nubbin provides splen-

did views and a satisfying feeling of accomplishment that far surpasses the actual effort involved. Overlooking nearby Sherbrooke and Wapta Lakes, it is an easily-attained summit making full use of a popular hiking trail to the abandoned fire lookout. In total elevation gain, the lookout is over half-way there already. Try from late June on.

Drive to Wapta Lake Picnic Area at the west end of Wapta Lake, British Columbia, 5.1 km west of the Continental Divide at Kicking Horse Pass.

Follow the Sherbrooke Lake trail, branching off right at 1.4 km to old Paget Lookout site (3.5 km). From the site grovel upslope (north) on slippery

shale plates, gaining 425 m en route to the obvious high point. It is that simple. Having reached Paget Peak with so little trouble, you may decide to continue north along the ridge for an additional hour, where a slightly higher viewpoint reveals a more complete panorama. Views include the glacier-hung north face of Mount Victoria,

Paget Peak. L site of old lookout.

Photo courtesy of the Canadian Parks Service

Mt. Ogden forms the backdrop for Sherbrooke Lake, seen here from the summit of Paget Peak.

snowy Mount Balfour and distant guardians of the Selkirk Range 80 km away. The imposing relief of Mount Stephen's north aspect towering almost 2000 m above the Kicking Horse flats is a particularly noteworthy feature of the landscape.

Paget Peak is a part, though just barely, of what geologists define as The Main Ranges. They are further subdivided into western and eastern sections. Geology and topography of Main Ranges is quite different to, and some would argue, more interesting than that of the younger Front Ranges. Watchful eyes may note a wider diversity of rock types and colours during ascents throughout the Main Ranges, one example being the hardest rock in the Rockies, Gog Quartzite.

In contrast to the Front Ranges, glaciers and icefields abound in the Main Ranges. This is due primarily to the multitude of high peaks along the backbone of the Rockies. These giants wring moisture from approaching storm systems which often hang up around them, resulting in a cooler, wetter climate. While on the subject of glaciers, some editions of the map show notable glaciation on the south- and east-facing slopes of Paget and nearby Mount Bosworth. This glacier no longer exists.

Paget Peak was first ascended by A.O. Wheeler and Reverend Dean Paget of Calgary, founding member of the Alpine Club of Canada.

MOUNT BURGESS 2599 m

Difficulty An easy scree ascent from Burgess Pass trail; South Peak difficult with exposure
Ascent time 2-4 hours
Height gain 1330 m
Map 82 N/8 Lake Louise, N/7 Golden

Mount Burgess is a quick and easy scramble benefiting from an excellent approach trail. It overlooks multi-braided Kicking Horse River Valley and the hamlet of Field to the south, with beautiful Emer-

ald Lake on the north side ringed by Mount Carnarvon, The President and The Vice-President. The vicinity is world-famous for the Burgess Shale Beds which have revealed many unique fossils of invertebrate life forms previously unknown to science. The route described takes you to the north, or lower summit. Reaching the marginally higher south peak is more challenging and requires route-finding skills, but is entirely feasible. Try this ascent from late July on.

Park at Burgess Pass trailhead on the north side of the Trans-Canada Highway, 0.4 km east of Field.

Follow the steep Burgess Pass trail, passing the only source of water in 20 minutes. Continue through cool, sombre forest and massive firs, crossing a short section of washed-out trail that has been rebuilt since the heavy spring rains of 1990. Shortly before reaching Burgess Pass, you emerge onto a huge avalanche slope a couple of hundred metres wide, and are treated to unobstructed views of Mount Stephen across Kicking Horse Valley. Of more concern, however, are the steep walls of Mount Burgess above you. Allow one hour of fast walking to here.

The open slopes up to the base of the objective are mostly bare with only limited scrub and stunted evergreens surviving. A wide gully immediately to the right of a large treed island hugging the base of this face is the route of ascent. This prominent gully is visible from the highway below, but suffers foreshortening as you stand immediately below and gaze up at it. Further to

the right the lower mountain flanks are also quite heavily-treed, but there are no indications of any reasonable way up. Once you plod up the rubble towards the face it will become clear where to go. The correct gully is comparatively low-angled and not difficult. Keep to the right once within its confines until it breaks out onto open scree below the north top.

South Peak Option

The intervening ridge to the main (south) peak is not without challenge. It is preferable to drop down into the rocky basin between north and south summits. Ascend a narrow gully towards the north end of the ridge which trends south to the main peak, then detour left (east) and descend slightly. This avoids the narrowest part of the final bit along the ridge. To bypass these exposed portions, you may have to traverse across ledgy slabs towards little gullies that lead more directly to the main peak. Sound confusing? The lower north peak provides the perfect location to assess and perhaps justify the excursion.

From Burgess Pass, route follows gully.
N north summit, S south summit.

Return to Burgess Pass by descending
the same gully you ascended; it is easy
to reach from the aforementioned
rocky basin between north and south
summits by contouring east. Any other
gullies are much steeper and are not
plausible descent routes.

Alexander Burgess was Commis-
sioner of Public Lands for Canada, 1897.

MOUNT CARNARVON 3040 m

Difficulty Difficult scrambling via
south ridge for final distance
Ascent time 3-6 hours
Height gain 1735 m
Map 82 N/7 Golden

Mount Carnarvon is possibly the best
scramble near Field. There is little scree,
a well-maintained approach trail and
pleasing surroundings. There is also a lot
of elevation gain. When travelling the

Trans-Canada Highway, glancing north
at a point some 12 km west of Field
reveals Mount Carnarvon rising like a
great pyramid to eclipse snow-capped
President and Vice-President peaks to
the right. With the striking image it
projects and quality of scramble offered,
Mount Carnarvon deserves more visits
than it presently receives. It is preferable
to carry an ice-axe on this ascent. Try
from mid-July on.

From Field drive 2.7 km west along the
Trans-Canada Highway to Emerald Lake
road and follow it for 8 km to Emerald
Lake parking lot.

The trailhead for Hamilton Lake is located on the west side of the parking lot
near the entrance. Hike 5.5 km to scenic
Hamilton Lake, the perfect place to catch
your breath after the unforgiving approach hike and to fortify muscles for the
remaining 900 m of elevation gain. Cross
the lake's outlet stream and ascend the

meadowy hillside which gives way to
brown shale and the south ridge. The
ridge can be followed most of its length
to the summit with few detours necessary. Steeper rock steps are typically
quite solid (by Rockies standards!) and
are refreshingly entertaining when tack-
led head-on. Easier options exist too —
detour left if required. The strata lie
horizontal or dip slightly inward;
handholds are abundant and dependable, making progress pleasurable.

The ascent route follows the left-hand skyline ridge.

A head-on view of Carnarvon's south ridge.

One hundred vertical metres below the top the character of the route changes. Walls rear up steeply. Here you must traverse left 75 to 100 m and ascend gullies to overcome this last section. It is entirely possible you may encounter snow in these gullies, and will therefore require an ice-axe. Upon topping out on the summit mass it is worthwhile noting your exact ascent gully; they may all look alike on the return trip. A short walk leads to the cairn and the often snow-clad summit.

Though much lower, Emerald Peak sitting immediately east of Hamilton Lake is an easy ascent as can be ascertained from this lofty perch. More spectacular is the large glaciated area of the Mummery Group to the north-west. Closer at hand is Mount Balfour and the Wapta Icefield. Incidentally, Wapta is a Stoney Indian word for river. Bearing this in mind, Wapta Lake loses much in the translation. Mount Carnarvon is named for Henry Howard Molyneux Herbert, Fourth Earl of Carnarvon, and parliamentary author of the British North America Act.

MOUNT STEPHEN 3199 m

Difficulty Difficult for final distance via south-west slopes; exposure
Ascent time 4-7 hours
Height gain 1920 m
Map 82 N/8 Lake Louise

Mount Stephen is a demanding ascent which requires route-finding and a measure of stamina above that of many other scrambles. It is the first Rockies peak above 3050 m of which there is irrefutable evidence of ascent. While employed by the Government to chart the railway's mountain section, McArthur and Riley struggled to the top, lugging heavy surveying impedimenta, in September of 1887. Though Tom Wilson claimed to have made a prior ascent, it was never substantiated.

The vertical relief between this brooding behemoth and Field is imposing, exhibiting a largely uninterrupted face towering 1900 m above. No doubt this loftiness accounts for a good part of the attention Mount Stephen receives today. The mountain is composed mainly of dolomites and shales laid down during the Devonian period some 550 million years ago. This era coincides with the first abundant fossils found in geological history. Examples litter lower flanks. Incidentally, removal of specimens is a punishable offense and is rigidly enforced by periodic and surprise checks. Try this ascent from mid-July on. An ice-axe is recommended.

Park at Stephen Fossil Beds trailhead near the creek at the end of First Street east in Field. Because of past thefts of fossils, climbers now require a Park permit and trail use is carefully monitored. Permits are available at Yoho Park Information Centre at the highway turn-off.

From the trailhead, an unrelenting grind takes you to the first indications of fossil beds in an hour and, not surprisingly, the path dwindles soon after. Only parties ascending the peak are given permission to pass through this area freely, with the understanding that they MUST NOT stop and search for souvenirs. Contravention of this regulation will prevent access entirely, so for the sake of future parties, please don't abuse the privilege.

Above the fossil beds continue up broken rock to a wide shoulder where again a path appears, wending its way over shale and scree towards a short

A long way up! S shoulder.

rockband. A gully cleaves this to your right. Continue up more scree. Behind you, a panorama of peaks unfolds. The distant, snow-capped Selkirks rise to the west, and to the north the President and Vice-President emerge.

The last 125 m of elevation gain requires route-finding through numerous short cliffs. Detour right to surmount most of the rockbands encountered. Innumerable cairns and wands clutter ledges, and you could conceivably spend the day merely traversing back and forth among these. Finally, after gaining the nearly horizontal summit ridge, an exposed traverse completes the ascent. This crest is NOT for anyone prone to vertigo. If the tedious trudge didn't leave you breathless, one quick glance down may do so — Field lies over one airy mile below. Since a stubborn cornice often clings to this drafty crest, you would be well-advised to save this endeavour for later in the summer. During one dry year, early July turned out to be a little too soon. Disappointed individuals were halted mere minutes short of success.

Mount Stephen is named for Scotsman George Stephen, later Lord Stephen, stalwart supporter and president of the Canadian Pacific Railway during its difficult formative years. Upon realizing that the peak was to bear his name, he reciprocated by adopting the title "Mount", thereby becoming Lord Mount Stephen, in what will surely stand throughout history as a unique case of name-swapping.

Descending the difficult upper section of Mt Stephen. Great fun!
Photo: Kris Thorsteinsson

NARAO PEAK 2974 m

Difficulty Moderate scrambling
along north ridge
Ascent time 4-6 hours
Height gain 1225 m
Map 82 N/8 Lake Louise

Narao Peak is a pleasant scramble proffering expansive views of several major summits along the Continental Divide. The north ridge is a long, enjoyable scramble, largely casual walking highlighted by short, horizontally-bedded rock steps. Because much of the west aspect is an uninteresting slope of scree flanked by forest, scramblers ascend the peak infrequently. Two steep, parallel ice couloirs on the north side are undoubtedly the most striking features. These couloirs generate interest among ice-climbing enthusiasts who ascend the mountain more often than anyone else. Although the ice couloirs are far more challenging, views along the scramblers route are far more scenic. Try from July on.

Drive to Lake O'Hara parking lot located at the west junction of Highway 1-A and the Trans-Canada Highway, 3.1 km west of Continental Divide and 1.5 km east of Wapta Lake service centre. Cross the railway tracks and turn right.

The initial challenge is to ascertain the path of least resistance through forest on the west slopes. This side is easily studied from the Trans-Canada Highway, and you may want to take time to do this.

Wander along the Lake O'Hara access road for a little less than 2 km. Bear left and make your way through bush to treeline and the north ridge itself. Small, crumbling cliffs interrupting the crest are all surmounted either head-on or by moving around to your right; none is very high. Shortly before the top, a gap-

A foreshortened view of Narao's north ridge. Lake O'Hara road out of sight to the right.

ing maw on your left signifies the exit point of Narao's north ice gully. The cairn lies a few minutes past this chasm.

Nearby is Mount Victoria's brooding icy north face; beyond, the mysterious Goodsirs preside over rarely visited Ice River and Ottertail valleys. Emerald waters of Sherbrooke Lake are overshadowed by a backdrop of glaciated peaks scattered across the southern end of Wapta Icefield. Mounts Balfour, Niles and Daly are among them.

If you choose to **descend** the north ridge in its entirety, note that just above treeline there is a 10 m-high cliff. Go around it slightly right of the end of the ridge. Below this, you have two options.

You can contour around into meadows of Popes/Narao cirque (481975) and by heading north, will emerge onto a broad scree ledge hugging the NE flanks of Narao Peak, several hundred metres above Ross Lake. This well-trodden ramp can be traversed north to a goat path (watch for flagging) which leads steeply down to the south end of Ross Lake below. A hiking trail

then connects from Ross Lake back to Lake O'Hara road.

If you prefer not to visit Popes/Narao cirque, from the end of the north ridge tramp back down the west slope into forest to regain Lake O'Hara road.

Certainly one of the stranger names bestowed upon a summit, Narao is reputed to mean "hit in the stomach" in the Stoney Indian language.

Descending the north ridge of Narao Peak.

Looking towards north-west summit of Mt. Yukness en route to south-east summit.

MOUNT YUKNESS 2847 m

Difficulty Easy scrambling to col and north-west summit; mainly moderate exposed scrambling to south-east (true) summit
Ascent time 2-3 hours
Height gain 810 m
Map 82 N/8 Lake Louise

Mount Yukness is a fine viewpoint in idyllic alpine surroundings almost unmatched anywhere in the Rockies. The biggest obstacle of this entire outing is actually getting to Lake O'Hara. Because It is a beautiful, fragile area, Yoho Park places strict controls on the number of visitors allowed there at any given time. Due to the difficulty in obtaining reservations, this is not a trip to plan on short notice. Although it is possible to ascend the peak and catch the bus out the same day, it is a shame to be tied to so tight a schedule. Try from July on.

Access to Lake O'Hara, the starting point, is via a 12 km bus ride (For more information about necessary bus/campsite reservations, contact Canadian Parks Service at 604-343-6324). Lake O'Hara parking lot is located at the west junction of Highway 1-A and the Trans-Canada Highway, 3.1 km west of the Continental Divide and 1.5 km east of Wapta Lake service centre. Cross the railway tracks and turn right. The bus runs daily from late June through late September. Biking in is not allowed.

Photo: Don Beers

Mt. Yukness. S south-east (higher) summit, C col, N north-west summit.

Photo: Kris Thorsteinsson

On a pinnacle near the true summit. Mt. Stephen behind.

From Lake O'Hara Lodge, hike along the south lakeshore and up the Opabin East trail to Opabin Lake at the south-east end of the plateau. From Opabin Lake signpost and trail junction it is relatively simple to scramble straight up the south side of Mount Yukness to a col between the two summits. Head up over rock steps where waterfalls trickle down, then angle diagonally up to the left below high cliffs, going through a gully to reach the final scree slopes above. You can also start 300 m along the left shore of Opabin Lake where an unsigned, deteriorating path diverges left from Opabin Pass trail. Cairns aid route-finding along the way. From Yukness Col, there are few problems preventing a visit to the lower north-west point.

The higher south-east peak involves some exposed scrambling on ledges to circumvent a pinnacle along the summit ridge, and is a more difficult undertaking. Once you reach the summit, the grandiose surroundings are certain to stir emotions. For anyone seized by an urge to yodel, the summit offers an ideal projection point providing no end of amusement. When facing Lake Oesa and Abbott Pass, multiple echoes reverberate in a natural amphitheatre formed by the quartzite walls of Mounts Yukness, Lefroy and Victoria. Remember, amid all the frivolity, that you may have to catch a bus yet. More reserved souls will appreciate the panorama with less fanfare.

Yukness is the Stoney Indian word for "sharpened" such as a knife — purely descriptive in this context. Similarly, Oesa means "ice", which covers the lake about thirteen months out of twelve.

ICEFIELDS PARKWAY AND JASPER

Mount Andromache	2996 m	moderate	p. 184
Dolomite Peak	2998 m	difficult	p. 185
Cirque Peak	2993 m	easy	p. 188
Observation Peak	3174 m	easy	p. 189
Mount Chephren	3307 m	difficult	p. 190
Nigel Peak	3211 m	moderate	p. 192
Mount Wilcox	2884 m	moderate	p. 194
Sunwapta Peak	3315 m	easy	p. 196
Pyramid Mountain	2763 m	easy	p. 198
Hawk Mountain	2553 m	difficult	p. 200
Roche Miette	2316 m	moderate	p. 202

The majority of peaks in this chapter border the Icefields Parkway which joins Banff National Park with neighbouring but larger Jasper National Park. The Icefields Parkway has been called the most scenic drive in the world. Year after year, awe-struck visitors ply its length by cycle, car, and bus. Each twist in the road reveals a new and better view of glistening glaciers and high, soaring summits. The finest scenery is perhaps found at Bow Lake towards the south end and near the Columbia Icefields which lie just north of the half-way point of this 245 km-long highway.

The Columbia Icefield is a 380 sq km frozen sea of glaciers and icefalls straddling the spine of the Rockies. Many of the highest summits are found here. Uniquely enough, it is the hydrographic apex of North America — a scholarly way of saying that the meltwater flows in three different compass directions and eventually empties into three major oceans. In the past, the spectacle has appeared in television commercials for products ranging from tires to beer.

Though many of the mountains along this road are steep technical ascents, there are a few easy ascents. One highly recommended scramble is Mount Wilcox which happens to be right across from the Columbia Icefields. It returns excellent views for the effort. If you head up the Icefields Parkway, keep in mind that the Columbia Icefield records in excess of 900 mm of annual precipitation — more than twice that of Banff or Jasper, and fifty percent more than even Lake Louise. No wonder so much ice prevails! Consider yourself blessed if you experience sunny weather in this area.

Besides the scrambles along the Parkway, I have included a couple just east of Jasper townsite on the Yellowhead Highway (Highway 16), a drier area. During bad weather, if you head east of Jasper you can frequently salvage a day in the mountains, rather like heading for Canmore or Kananaskis

181

when Lake Louise socks in.

Access The region is accessed by the Icefields Parkway (Highway 93) which begins immediately west of Lake Louise from the Trans-Canada Highway and travels north-west for 240 km to the town of Jasper. Intersecting the Parkway is David Thompson Highway (Highway 11). This alternate access route leads east from Saskatchewan River Crossing to Red Deer. Jasper can also be reached by the Yellowhead Highway (Highway 16) which runs from Edmonton to Prince George, B.C. Brewster operates a daily shuttle between Calgary International Airport and Jasper, and Via Rail also stops in Jasper from Edmonton. Greyhound buses travel through the town en route from B.C. to Edmonton, but to do anything besides tramp around town, you need a car.

Facilities Since the only businesses along the Parkway are mostly "wide spots in the road" generally catering to tourists (with money!), you should probably buy your supplies and gas at either Lake Louise or Jasper. Gas is available at Columbia Icefields, Sunwapta Falls and Saskatchewan River Crossing, but expect to pay more. Jasper, on the other hand, has everything you will need. For equipment, see Totem Men's Wear and Ski Shop — they also rent some gear. Environment Canada maintains a weather office in the town, if the Park Information Centre's forecasts aren't to your liking! Entertainment as diverse as gondola lifts and hot springs await nearby, the latter being fairly close to Roche Miette — a scramble in the dry Front Ranges east of Jasper. Gas, snacks and limited facilities are found at Pocahontas on Highway 16 if you're out that way. Co-incidentally, this is also the turn-off for Miette Hot Springs.

Accommodation Scattered throughout the length of the Parkway are numerous campgrounds and hostels. All are popular. Lodges, cabins, and chalets along the way are typically expensive. There are two campgrounds adjacent to the Icefields; Icefields Campground, the smaller and closer of the two forbids both trailers and motor homes, so it is a natural choice for cyclists and climbers. It isn't unusual for folks to share or sublease part of a tent pad here when space is at a premium! Wilcox Campground sits a kilometre or two farther south. Around Jasper, Wapiti and Whistlers are big campgrounds and lie just south of town — the latter boasts showers. For peaks along Highway 16, Snaring River and Pocahontas campgrounds are closest. The nearest hostel to Jasper is Whistler Hostel, 5 km south of the town on Whistlers road. If you're looking for hotels, motels, and the like, there are plenty around.

Information Along the Icefields Parkway, the only information centre is right beside the highway near the Athabasca Glacier toe at Columbia Icefields. The Park boundary lies just south of here. Staff behind the counter are very helpful regarding climbing and scrambling routes. Besides this centre and the one in Lake Louise, there is also a Parks Info Centre in Jasper, housed in a rustic building close to the train station on Connaught Drive. Watch for the largest patch of grass along the main drag — that's where you'll find it. Like their counterparts at the Icefields booth, staff are congenial and quick to offer details about nearby scrambles.

Wardens Warden offices are located near Saskatchewan River Crossing, at Sunwapta Falls, just east of Jasper and in Lake Louise village.

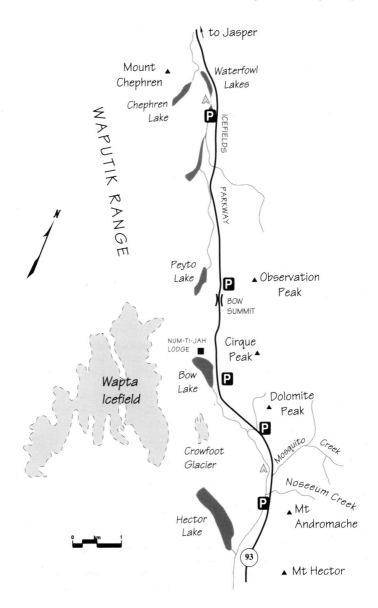

to Jasper

Mount Chephren ▲

Waterfowl Lakes

Chephren Lake

WAPUTIK RANGE

ICEFIELDS PARKWAY

Peyto Lake

▲ Observation Peak

BOW SUMMIT

NUM-TI-JAH LODGE ■

Cirque Peak ▲

Bow Lake

▲ Dolomite Peak

Wapta Icefield

Mosquito Creek

Noseeum Creek

Crowfoot Glacier

Hector Lake

▲ Mt Andromache

93

▲ Mt Hector

0   km   1

MOUNT ANDROMACHE 2996 m

Difficulty Moderate via north-west scree slopes and ridge
Ascent time 3-5 hours
Height gain 1140 m
Map 82 N/9 Hector Lake (492182)

Mount Andromache (An-DROM-akee) is an easily approached peak alongside the Icefields Parkway which gives good views of Hector Glacier. Because the name is unofficial, and therefore unmarked on the map, it does not fall into the category of well-known objectives, but that shouldn't stop the true peak-bagger. After all, the approach distance is paltry and the views are superb. You can also effect a traverse towards Mount Hector, crossing a higher unnamed point along the way. Try from July on.

Park on the Icefields Parkway at Noseeum Creek, 22.2 km north of the Trans-Canada Highway, 1.3 km south of Mosquito Creek.

Gain the broad and rapidly deteriorating north ridge directly above the parking spot. Scramblers should avoid straying left onto the diminutive Molar Glacier, and instead proceed up laborious scree. Work slightly left at a steep wall then continue towards the summit ridge.

A slightly higher unnamed peak to the east can be reached without trouble in 30 minutes. Contrary to what some map editions indicate, Molar Icefield no longer covers the intervening ridge.

Descent Traversing to this unnamed peak places you in a favourable position to continue to Hector Pass (510168) by descending scree to the south-east. Just below the pass short cliffs above a sink-hole may be problematic. By gaining a small amount of elevation and rounding a talus shoulder to the southwest these rockbands can be circumvented. Continue the descent by pursuing the right-hand side of the drainage until a waterfall makes it more logi-cal to traverse to your right onto open slopes, then drop down and regain Hector Creek for the final jaunt back to the Parkway. Allow 8-10 hours for the entire circuit, including the two kilometre walk back to your vehicle.

The traverse might well be preferable if reversed. The rubble at the north end of Andromache is so disgustingly loose it would be easier in descent.

In Greek mythology, Andromache was wife to the noble hero Hector; in Canadian mountain lore, however, Mount Hector commemorates Dr. James Hector of the Palliser Expedition whose wife was not Andromache, which perhaps explains the absence of official endorsement for this epithet.

A Andromache, H Hector, U unnamed, D Hector Pass descent.

DOLOMITE PEAK 2998 m

Difficulty Difficult. Route-finding skills helpful
Ascent time 3-5 hours
Height gain 1100 m
Map 82 N/9 Hector Lake

Dolomite Peak is a highly recommended scramble which reserves the best part for last. Rock is generally firm, and summit views can only be described as spectacular. Dolomite is an altered (and improved) form of limestone, appreciated by climbers due to its dependable nature. In this area it occurs in a particular geological formation called the Lyell Formation which makes up the top 300 or so metres of this castellated mountain. Like the range for which it is named, but in contrast to much of the Rockies, Dolomite Peak offers surprisingly firm rock, at least on the upper walls where steep towers present exhilarating scrambling — quite different than what a casual inspection might suggest. Since the strata are bedded almost horizontally, so too, are the ledges. This makes the last few hundred metres particularly delightful. Try the ascent from July on.

Dolomite Peak. Route ascends gully between 3rd and 4th (highest) tower.

Begin at Helen Creek, 28.5 km north of the Trans-Canada Highway on the Icefields Parkway. A small gravel parking area exists at the north end of the bridge. Approach is via the winter route to Helen Lake/Dolomite Pass.

As you proceed along the trail you should note the specific outline of the tower which you are aiming for since there are so many. The highest point is the fourth pinnacle from the north. You may want to drive further north to deter-mine the exact shape of this one. After about 25 minutes you come to the second avalanche slope, five minutes beyond the first stream crossing. In spring 1991 the bridge was washed out by unusually high water levels, but even without the convenience of a bridge the crossing is straightforward. There are an infinite number of ways to plod up the extensive open slopes which comprise the lower flanks. One way is a plod up the left side of a usually-dry watercourse on steep but not overly loose shale slopes which typify most routes. Sporadic cliffs break the monotony of this section, but pose no problems.

Upon reaching the base of the actual summit mass, you must traverse north (left) towards the gully between peaks three and four. This chute provides access to peak four, the highest point. You can either continue to walk along the base of steep walls all the way to the 3-4 gully, or watch for the first suitable place

Typical scrambling near the top of Dolomite Peak.

to scramble up to gain the broad scree ledge system running the length of the peak and wander along it.

Once you're directly beneath these towers, foreshortening renders it puzzling to decide which one is which. The fourth tower is wider than either the third one or the fifth; the right-hand side of the second tower flaunts an impossibly steep and smooth buttress probing the skyline — this is perhaps the most recognizable feature of any pinnacle from this abbreviated perspective.

The proper gully should be the widest one you come to. Ascend this gully to just past the spot where a large chunk of rock protrudes through the channel of debris like a shark's fin, then gain good ledges on the right-hand side. Work your way around to the right on these ledges in a rising traverse into another smaller gully. A further few minutes of steep but enjoyable scrambling leads to the double summit of the fourth and highest peak. There's plenty of room for route variation hereabouts and the rock is sound. Ledges are substantial but not entirely rubble-free — a helmet would not be out of place, especially if you are with a group.

Peak three can also be reached from the vicinity of the aforementioned "shark's fin" in the gully. Traverse north (left) on a wide scree ledge and scramble a short distance up rock steps to the top. Though it may appear possible to reach peak three from the top of the gully, access is barred by a notch so you must start lower down.

The views from Dolomite Peak encompass the total spectrum of mountain landscape, from drab, crumbling peaks to the east, to shining glacier-clad summits piercing the Wapta Icefield in the west. Between lie the emerald greens and azure blues of alpine meadows and

Photo: Kris Thorsteinsson

A successful party waves from tower #4.

lakes. Dominant mountains include Balfour, Willingdon, Chephren and Temple. Even distant Mount Assiniboine is visible on a clear day. A camera is a must.

The quickest **descent** is straight down directly below the 3-4 gully to Helen Creek. Fine shale slopes make for a fast run. A few short bluffs interrupt the bee-line to tree-line, but these pose only moderate difficulties and are descended with a little bit of searching about — usually by traversing left (south). Expect the entire return trip to take less than half the ascent time.

In 1899 Dolomite Peak was named for its resemblance to the European Dolomites by Ralph Edwards, a well-schooled English transplant who was periodically employed by Banff packer Tom Wilson. On this occasion, he was accompanying "dudes" on a climbing and exploration trip up Pipestone River towards Siffleur River and the Bow Lake environs. Today, adjacent Mounts Thompson, Noyes, and Weed commemorate members of the excursion. Lakes Helen and Katherine near Dolomite Pass were named after daughters of a fourth member, Harry Nicholls.

187

CIRQUE PEAK 2993 m

Difficulty An easy ascent, largely hiking, via south slopes
Ascent time 3-5 hours
Height gain 1050 m
Map 82 N/9 Hector Lake

Cirque Peak is a virtually fool-proof ascent reached by a popular trail in classic alpine surroundings. There are no difficulties; in fact, the ascent is sometimes done in winter. Views include nearby icefields and distant ranges, including Mount Assiniboine, almost 70 km away. Try from July on.

Drive to Helen Lake/Dolomite Pass trailhead on the the Icefields Parkway, 33.2 km north of the Trans-Canada Highway and 7.8 km south of Bow Summit. Parking lot is on the east side of the road.

Hike the well-graded trail for 6 km to Helen Lake. Tempting though it may be to merely fritter away a day lounging in luxuriant alpine meadows by Helen Lake, greater rewards await you from the easily-attained summit of Cirque Peak. Amble over to the shaly south slopes and tackle (or detour around) a rocky outcrop near the base. Then follow your nose. With every metre gained a correspondingly wider panorama of glaciated Wapta Icefields unfolds to the west. To the south-east lies Mount Hector draped under a blanket of ice. A ski ascent of this glacier is a popular undertaking for winter mountaineers bent on bagging eleven-thousand footers.

The east peak of Cirque is marginally higher and probably still has a register. Allow 1.5 hours from Helen Lake for your ascent; less than half that for the rapid descent. The name "Cirque" is purely a description of the amphitheatre formed by adjacent peaks.

Cirque Peak is an easy ascent in a lovely alpine setting. From Helen Lake , route ascends scree slopes of the facing south ridge.

OBSERVATION PEAK 3174 m

Difficulty easy/moderate scrambling via west slopes
Ascent time 3-6 hours
Height gain 1100 m
Map 82 N/9 Hector Lake

Much of the west side of Observation Peak is scree, particularly south of the described route, consequently sundry possibilities exist to approach the upper environs. We chose to follow up an obvious wide gully which is slightly south of the false summit. Try from late June on.

Park on an old gravel road on the east side of the Icefields Parkway at the crest of Bow Summit, 41 km north of the Trans-Canada Highway.

Walk just past a right-angle bend, then follow a major gully left of an avalanche zone and bush. Short cliffs at half-height, barely noticeable from the valley, look problematic as you approach but are easily circumvented around the right side on ledges — watch for cairns here. Alternatively, these diversions could be avoided entirely by starting your ascent slightly further south, thereby rendering the venture entirely without challenge. Continue up the ridge to a false summit, keeping an eye out for large cornices which overhang the east side. A brief descent and 20 min-

utes plodding north-west brings you to the spacious summit some 100 m higher.

Charles Noyes, a Boston clergyman who made several Rockies first ascents, including those of nearby Cirque Peak and Mount Balfour, felt it was one of the best viewpoints his party had attained on their exploratory foray of 1899. Who can argue even today. A careful squint will distinguish several significant peaks such as Sir Donald, Mount Forbes, Assiniboine, and Mount Hector, yet it is not these mighty monarchs which most thoroughly satisfy the senses but the milky-blues of nearby Peyto and Bow Lakes which bestow a feeling of sublime tranquillity.

G gully, F false summiit. True summit is to left.

MOUNT CHEPHREN 3307 m

Difficulty Difficult for a short distance only; ice-axe suggested.
Ascent time 5-9 hours (in dry conditions; no snow)
Height gain 1630 m
Map 82 N/15 Mistaya Lake

Mount Chephren is a stunning eye-catcher situated along the Icefields Parkway — one of the most scenic drives in the world. This description is due chiefly to an abundance of majestic mountains, although most are not as accessible as this one. Unequalled panoramas await the successful scrambler.

The massive height and location of this pyramidal giant necessitate a high degree of respect. Though both Mounts Temple and Stephen slightly surpass Chephren's total elevation gain, the latter's approach is more time consuming. Chephren Lake hiking trail seems unnecessarily long and

indirect, which it is, and only a marginal path exists along the left-hand (east) shore of the lake itself. The right-hand shore is wicked bushwhacking — to be avoided at all costs. As well, some fairly steep scrambling is involved in surmounting the first cliff band, especially if you neglect to scout out the easiest place! But the views...here Chephren dominates the heights.

Due to the length of this route an early start, perhaps by headlamp, is encouraged. That way you should be well up those bone-dry south-facing slopes before the full heat of the day hits and saps your energy. The best time to attempt this peak is well into summer, about late July and through August, when steep grey-black cliffs and gullies on the south side should be completely free of snow and ice. For fit individuals equipped with an ice-axe the ascent is highly recommended.

Begin at Chephren Lake trailhead at the south-west end of Waterfowl Lakes Campground on the Icefields Parkway, 57.4 km north of the Trans-Canada Highway, or 19.7 km south of Saskatchewan River Crossing. Drive through the campground to the west end and park near the footbridge across Mistaya River.

Follow the Chephren Lake hiking trail to the lake in about an hour, and muddle your way down the left shore through forest and across rockslides. Arrive at the second inlet stream at the west end in another hour or so. Some people camp by this silty stream and take two days for the outing. This is not really required although you may want to wet your whistle here — it could be the last water and the real elevation gain has yet to start.

Either hike along the right side or gain the awkward steep crest of the lateral moraine leading towards the Chephren/White Pyramid col. Walk along this only a short distance to grassy, south-facing slopes — tasty little blueberries here — then diverge right to follow a dry watercourse up the open hillside. Higher up this drainage splits; notice that the left branch leads towards an obvious drainage scar breaking the lowest cliff band. Either here or some 75-100 m further left are the best spots to surmount this initial hurdle. The greenish rock is steep but solid. As you progress, it is worth looking back down periodically to recognize the terrain on descent. Otherwise it appears a bit intimidating on return.

The next wall confronting you is a vertical black band about 20 m high.

Photo: Bruno Engler

South slopes showing route of ascent. To left is White Pyramid with Chephren/White Pyramid col at centre.

Traverse left on scree along the base of it for 100 m or so and ascend an easy gully of light brown rock. Contour further left again over a rounded scree shoulder until the Chephren/White Pyramid col is visible. You now have a choice of either skirting north-west along the foot of a short cliff and plodding summit-ward from that point, or you can gradually angle up left over short snow patches and rock steps. A little chute cleaves the only wall of any consequence. Words cannot describe the wearisome stretch of loose rubble near the summit ridge.

A brief walk leads to the cairn and register.

Major peaks visible on a clear day include Mount Columbia — second highest elevation in the Rockies, Mount Forbes, The Lyells, The Goodsirs and even the Howser Towers of the Purcell Range, 75 km distant. The most awe-inspiring panorama, though, lies just left of nearby White Pyramid — a multitude of glaciated summits awash in a sea of ice, collectively known as The Freshfields.

Chephren (Kef-ren) was the builder of the second of the great pyramids of Egypt; the mountain was once known as Pyramid mountain, but was renamed in 1918 due to one already so-named overlooking Jasper townsite.

NIGEL PEAK 3211 m

Difficulty Moderate scrambling, much scree and perhaps snow slopes via south-west side to north ridge; Ice-axe suggested.
Ascent time 2.5-5 hours
Height gain 1175 m
Map 83 C/3 Columbia Icefield

Nigel Peak is usually overlooked in favour of bigger objectives, but for a non-technical ascent few summit views can compare, including those granted by larger peaks to the west. When bigger peaks like nearby Athabasca and Andromeda are clouded in, climbers may be able to salvage the day with this ascent. Try from July on.

Nigel Peak showing route from Wilcox Pass trail. B North-west bowl, N north ridge.

Park at the entrance to Wilcox Campground on the Icefields Parkway, 2.7 km south of Columbia Icefield Chalet. The trail to Wilcox Pass starts here.

Follow Wilcox Pass trail for about five minutes to an opening in the forest, then hike up the steep hillside, aiming for Nigel Peak. Cross undulating meadows towards scree slopes on the south-west side of a subsidiary ridge trending northwest from point 878868. Stay left of the stream which drains the summit mass and flows through Wilcox Campground. Tedious scree slopes occasionally relent by way of waterworn slabs. This is more apparent as you near the crest above where the terrain also steepens. The top of this ridge makes a fine rest stop.

A rounded saddle connects to the main mass of the peak. Trudge up this — possible cornice on the right — making minor detours left at rotten rock steps. Snow lingers into August some years on this shaded slope, and as you must traverse either across or above it to attain the north ridge, an ice-axe is invaluable. The slopes descending towards the tiny snowfield below are lengthy.

Although there have been ascents straight up the north-west bowl, rocks are often damp while ledges hide under precarious piles of stones. Traversing further over to gain the north ridge offers a safer option. It is not necessary to set foot on the minor glacier clinging to the left side of this ridge, but should the ridge also be snow-covered you should at least be aware of its presence.

At least twenty-two of the Rockies' fifty-odd 11,000' (3353 m) peaks are distinguishable from the summit. Mount Robson qualifies as the most distant. Mount Bryce, although seen from nearby Mount Wilcox, is entirely hidden behind Andromeda from this angle.

Some parties reach the north ridge route by hiking along Wilcox Pass and circumventing the rock "wing" around the north end. This is a more circuitous approach that does little to eliminate the ever-present scree.

Although descents towards the shaly basin feeding the creek draining to Wilcox Campground look plausible, banks of the stream are composed of steep hard dirt and gravelly slabs, rendering the experience unpleasant.

Nigel Vavasour was the guide who accompanied climbers and explorers J. Norman Collie and Hugh Stutfield on their nearby explorations of 1897, which included the discovery of the expansive Columbia Icefield.

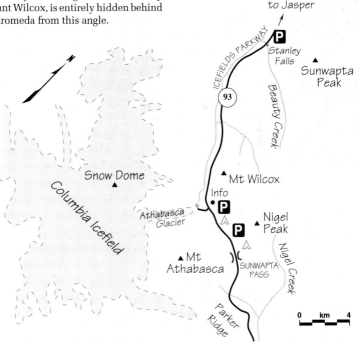

MOUNT WILCOX 2884 m

Difficulty Moderate scrambling via south-east ridge, mild exposure near the top
Ascent time 1.5-4 hours depending on starting point
Height gain 900 m
Map 83 C/3 Columbia Icefield

Mount Wilcox pales in elevation compared to neighbours Athabasca, Andromeda and Kitchener, but its strategic location and ease of ascent makes it far more accessible to the average hiker or scrambler. When the weather co-operates, it offers possibly the best view in the entire Rockies for the energy expended. If, while in the area, you do nothing else, at least scramble up this peak. Try from July on.

Icefields Parkway at Sunwapta Pass. Begin either directly behind the Icefields Information Centre or at Wilcox Campground and Wilcox Pass trailhead, 2.7 km to the south.

The most direct approach lies immediately behind the Icefields Information Centre. Scramble up whatever weakness in the rockband suits your fancy to reach rolling alpine terrain above. An approach via Wilcox Pass hiking trail is slightly longer, but judging by the register entries many scramblers

do arrive that way. From the broad environs of the pass, gain the southeast ridge and follow a fairly well-worn path which keeps just below the crest. Cairns exist but are superfluous. Only a couple of sections involve any hands-on scrambling, and towards the top there is some mild exposure. In general, keep right at any narrow bits.

Views along the entire route are praiseworthy, in particular those of Athabasca Glacier and the snocoaches full of tourists which ply its surface. From the top one could spend

Approaching Mt. Wilcox from Wilcox Pass. Ascent follows left-hand ridge.

Photo: Gillean Daffern

Enjoying the scene from the summit.
Mts. Athabasca and Andromeda (left to right)
above the Athabasca Glacier.

a considerable time with map and compass attempting to identify each peak. The icy mass between Mount Athabasca and Snow Dome is Mount Bryce, a much-sought after but seldom-climbed summit.

Walter Wilcox, a scholar of Yale, did considerable exploring in the Lake Louise area in company of fellow students Samuel Allen and Lewis Frissell about 1893. The name was suggested by British alpinist John Norman Collie whose explorations in the Rockies from 1897 to 1911 added appreciably to the limited information then available.

SUNWAPTA PEAK 3315 m

Difficulty Easy scrambling via south-west slopes
Ascent time 4-6 hours
Height gain 1735 m
Map 83 C/6 Sunwapta Peak

Sunwapta Peak is a deceiving ascent taking significantly longer than highway glances suggest. Besides an ice-axe for snow lingering on the upper slopes, no special equipment is required — just perseverance. Try from July on.

Drive 15.6 km north of Sunwapta Pass (2 km south of Beauty Creek Hostel) to Stanley Falls hiking trail sign and pull-off area on the east side of the Icefields Parkway. There is a less foreshortened view of the mountain about 2 km south.

From the pull-off spot, the trail curves over into the trees to a paved section of old highway. Do not follow the road south to Stanley Falls, but instead walk north (left) along it for a few minutes to the first stream. The road is barricaded here by a pile of gravel. As seen from the road, this watercourse is the more southerly of two parallel drainages.

Follow the left-hand side of the drainage, encountering short stretches of deadfall and hints of a trail, until you

reach tree-line. Once in the open, angle right and continue up lengthy rubble slopes which often hold snow well into the summer. This upper section, appearing so inconsequential from the road, never seems to end. It is hardly surprising — there are some 1000 vertical metres between tree-line and the summit cairn! Despite the drudgery, the remainder is largely a walk, an occasional backward glance towards Mounts Woolley, Diadem and Alberta doing much to ease the grind.

Sunwapta is a Stoney Indian word for turbulent water in reference to the nearby river, and was used by Professor A.P. Coleman during his exploits in the area around the turn of the century.

South-west slopes of Sunwapta Peak.

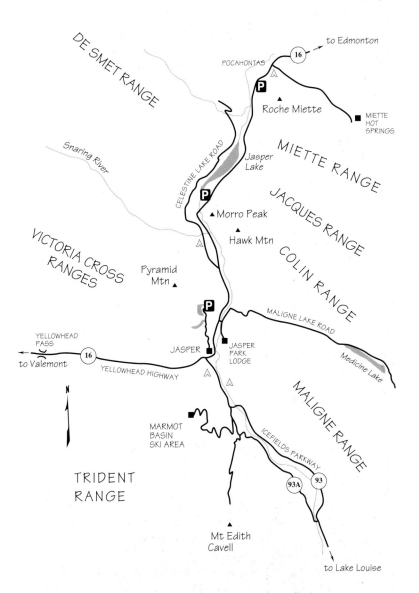

DE SMET RANGE

to Edmonton

16

POCAHONTAS

P

Roche Miette

MIETTE HOT SPRINGS

Snaring River

Jasper Lake

MIETTE RANGE

JACQUES RANGE

P

Morro Peak

Hawk Mtn

COLIN RANGE

VICTORIA CROSS RANGES

Pyramid Mtn

P

MALIGNE LAKE ROAD

JASPER

JASPER PARK LODGE

Medicine Lake

YELLOWHEAD PASS

16

to Valemont

YELLOWHEAD HIGHWAY

MALIGNE RANGE

N

MARMOT BASIN SKI AREA

ICEFIELDS PARKWAY

TRIDENT RANGE

93A 93

Mt Edith Cavell

to Lake Louise

PYRAMID MOUNTAIN 2763 m

Difficulty Easy scrambling
via north ridge
Height gain 1585 m
Ascent time Allow a full day for the
round trip
Map 83 D/16 Jasper

Pyramid Mountain is the guardian of Jasper and a good scramble to boot. The summit grants a commanding view of the Jasper environs and is a popular ascent with locals despite a ponderous telecommunications building and microwave tower hogging the summit. The rock is quartzite, not limestone. Rather than slogging up loose scree, you will find yourself clambering over big solid blocks — great fun going up but more time-consuming than scree coming down. Given the 11 km tram access road, the sensible approach is by mountain bike (rentals available in Jasper). Put your partner up for collateral if need be — it will be worth it for the ride down! Try from late June on.

Leave Jasper main street (Connaught Drive) and head north on Pine Avenue which becomes Pyramid Lake Drive. Continue past Pyramid Lake and park at the picnic area near the locked access gate some 7 km from the townsite.

Pyramid Mountain, showing the view from where you first gain the north ridge from the cirque. North ridge on the right. For variety, the left skyline ridge may be descended.

Photo: Gillean Daffern

From the parking area the road crosses the outlet stream from Pyramid Lake and begins a gradual climb through a forest of Douglas fir, spruce and lodgepole pine. After crossing a bridge the route jogs east, granting a view of the objective, then grinds its way to a junction. The right fork leads to The Palisade; follow the left fork. A myriad of culverts and switchbacks later (last reliable water at last culvert), the road eases up to the lower tram station. Unfortunately, you can't ride the tram — only persons working on the microwave equipment up top have that luxury!

Either wander along the track in its entirety as it winds left from the tram station into the cirque, or take a shortcut through a narrow gap in the trees to the right of the station. There is a tiny stream here and

Photo: Gillean Daffern   *Typical terrain on the north ridge*

a trail along the left bank. Higher up, cross to the right bank, then hike up meadow, aiming for a stony gully which leads to another break in the trees below where you regain the track.

At the point where the track ends at the edge of the grassy cirque, a faint trail continues up and left. Head for the crest of the north ridge above, aiming for a grass island on the left side of a broad ridge descending to the cirque mouth. Beyond this grass island, vague and various paths usher you through shallow gullies and rocky terrain to the ridge crest proper.

The broad ridge rises in steps, offering close-up views of the often snow-covered north-east face as you clamber up black lichen-encrusted boulders. Slabby sections can be detoured as required, until finally you top out on a

flat platform where monstrous man-made intrusions await. From the summit, many lakes in the area are visible although to mountain lovers, perhaps ice-clad Edith Cavell or the steeply-tilted Colin Range hold more intrigue. The summit serves as a jumping-off point for a multi-day scramble extending west towards Elysium Pass, incorporating peaks such as Cairngorm and Mount Henry en route. I do not have first-hand knowledge of this excursion; Jasper Wardens may be of help.

Most parties **return** the same way, although it is possible to descend the steeper east ridge bordering the opposite side of the triangular north-east face. Pyramid Mountain becomes a more appropriate name when viewed from the Athabasca Valley to the east. At one time it had been known as Priest's Rock.

199

HAWK MOUNTAIN 2553 m

Difficulty Moderate except for 5 m of difficult slab scrambling via west face and north-west ridge; some route-finding required
Ascent time 3-5 hours
Height gain 1500 m
Map 83 E/1 Snaring River

Hawk Mountain is a deservedly popular scramble in the Colin Range north-east of Jasper. The Colin Range, named for Colin Fraser of Hudson Bay Company, is typical Front Range topography. Steeply-tilted, slabby limestone faces are the norm; ridges are often long, undulating and sometimes quite exposed. Hawk Mountain is one of the more accessible peaks in this range, and can be attempted from about mid-June on.

From Jasper, follow the Yellowhead Highway (Highway 16) north-east towards Edmonton for 20 km. Park at a pull-off spot at the east end of the bridge over the Athabasca River.

From the parking spot by the end of the bridge, go up the dirt bank where a beaten path exists, mainly due to rock climbers visiting training climbs on Morro Peak. This trail, interestingly enough, is part of the historic Overlanders Route of 1862. The Overlanders were an adventurous group of 150 hardy souls who journeyed through here from Ontario to the B.C. Interior long before heading out west became fashionable.

Follow the trail some 40 minutes as it contours south above the valley floor to intersect Morro Creek drainage, the first one you reach. Hike up the right side of this often-dry stream through a burnt area to a point that allows you to gaze down into a canyon complete with a splashing waterfall. A well-trodden goat/sheep/occasional human trail rises gently off to the right, keeping roughly midway between brown slabs above and blackened timber below. This trail wanes on a shaly hillside overlooking a more southerly drainage at 281750.

From here, hike straight up towards the slabby face, going through a short belt of trees and clambering up a sizeable slope of broken rubble leading to the first band of grey slabs. The key to the entire route lies in finding the difficult 3 m-high chimney which cleaves these slabs. It can be identified by a dead stump at its left side. (The chimney itself is more awkward than are the slabs to the right.)

200

Route follows skyline ridge from left to right. C crux chimney.

Above the chimney an eroded trail hastens directly upwards. Grovel up this dirt to the base of more slabs where the path rises diagonally to the right and within minutes easily overcomes this band of slabs also.

Continue up steep terrain on an obvious path and enter heavy forest. There is usually a cairn or five here, as this is a critical area to recognize on the return. Evidently, everyone wants to construct his own landmark, and you may want to as well if there is room. Otherwise, you should at least familiarize yourself more completely with this particular spot so you can identify it on the descent. The section you have just completed can be termed the crux as now you are on the very backbone of the mountain and it would take some doing to go wrong.

Hike through timber along the ridge and, in some 20 minutes emerge onto slabs, rough and water-worn through eons of wind-driven rain. The summit is visible but still distant. When the ridge peters out, descend slightly and gain the next one over — some pleasant scrambling here onto the main spine leading directly to the summit.

Curiously, there are numerous quartzite boulders perched willy-nilly along this mass of limestone. They look entirely out of place and they are. These "erratics" have been transported from further west (Edith Cavell is quartzitic) by ancient glaciers which then deposited them in unlikely spots like this one. As the inquisitive sightseer once asked: Where has the glacier gone now?...Back for more rocks.

Climbers continue to be surprised upon seeing remains of a moose skeleton lying on the north ridge of Hawk Mountain in the direction of Mount Colin. Nobody will ever know what drove a gangly swamp-lover to wander so far from lowlands onto technical rock.

Descent From the summit it appears feasible to traverse partway towards the Hawk/Colin col, then descend south to 320730 and follow a treed ridge north-west back to the burned area and the second drainage to the south at 284750. Otherwise, return the same way, watching carefully for the specific point to descend the west face slabs.

Opposite: Looking towards the summit. Here the route crosses over to slabs and climbs onto the ridge crest.

ROCHE MIETTE 2316 m

Difficulty A moderate to difficult
scramble via north-east face
Ascent time 2-4 hours
Height gain 1425 m
Map 83 F/4 Miette

Roche Miette's vertical walls have stirred
emotions since bygone days when
voyageurs plied the waters of nearby
Athabasca River. In spite of its dramatic
west face the peak is not a particularly
demanding ascent. Benefiting from a
beaten path, this scramble is one of the
more frequented outings in the region,
serving also as the climbers descent
route. Try from June on.

Follow Yellowhead Highway (Highway 16) north-east from Jasper townsite towards Edmonton for 40 km, or 3.5 km south-west of Pocahontas, to a gravel access road on the south side of the highway. Park at the locked gate near an oil pipeline control valve just off the highway.

From the gravel access road, ignore the pipeline control valve just beyond the locked gate and follow the track northeast for 10 minutes. Watch carefully for a good trail which diverges right (cairn here), and follow this spur. Soon you cross the more easterly of two drainages originating below Roche Miette's north end. The path ascends hastily; take the right fork at the first intersection and left at the next one. In about one hour you emerge on open slopes revealing the mighty Athabasca winding east beyond Disaster Point towards rolling woodlands.

The high point of this ridge offers a delightful panorama and a good place to eye-ball the rest of the route. A faint trail angles left from the connecting saddle to a gully cleaving the first cliff band. Successive bands are similarly short. Most are easily overcome by traversing left to convenient gullies which allow you to ascend these obstacles with minimal fuss and only moderate scrambling. A pleasant option is to angle left onto clean slabs for the finish. There is some exposure to contend with but the rock is reliable.

The top of Roche Miette is a broad, undulating plateau hosting tiny mosses, hardy alpine flowers and scattered patches of grass which provide nourishment for Bighorn Sheep that sometimes graze here. The summit awaits 15 minutes south-east over a small hump. For those with time and energy to waste, two slightly higher points lying south can be ascended from the col between them. They involve only a bit of steep scrambling but are hardly worth it.

The usual view of Roche Miette from Highway 16.

Photo: Tony Daffern

The easy side. R ridge, S saddle, F first cliff band.

The west one is especially rotten and may have collapsed by the time this goes to press.

The summit block of Roche Miette is composed entirely of a particularly erosion-resistant limestone known as the Palliser Formation, a formation which constitutes the steepest cliffs of many peaks throughout the Canadian Rockies. You may also notice the odd lichen-clad quartzite boulder resting innocuously here and there. As on Mount Hawk closer to Jasper townsite, these glacially-transported specimens originated further west in the Main Ranges where quartzite peaks like Edith Cavell and The Ramparts stand guard. When the period of glaciation ended these erratics were left high and dry, sometimes on limestone summits like this one.

Miette was a legendary French Canadian voyageur with enviable qualities for tolerating the hardships of travel, was also known for his ability with the fiddle and as a teller of tall tales. When taunted by comrades about climbing the mountain now bearing his name, he responded to the dare by doing just that, dangling his legs over the precipice while contentedly puffing his pipe — or so the story goes. Roche is a French word meaning "rock".

Anticline: Inverted trough-shaped fold in mountain strata. Opposite shape to a syncline.

Arête: Narrow connecting ridge, either snow or rock.

Bergschrund: The crevasse formed between the edge of a body of snow and a rock mass.

Bivouac: A temporary, sometimes unplanned encampment.

Bushwhack: Thrash through bush without benefit of a trail.

Buttress: A column-like feature of rock on a mountain.

Cairn: Pile of rocks usually indicating route or top of a peak.

Castellated: Castle-shaped.

Chimney: A chimney-like feature on a rock face, often climbed using a technique of counter-pressure called stemming.

Cirque: Glacially-carved basin enclosed in steep, high walls.

Col: The crest of a mountain pass between two peaks.

Cornice: An overhanging edge of snow at the crest of a mountain peak or ridge caused by drifting.

Couloir: A steeply ascending gully or gorge in a mountain side which may be filled with snow or ice.

Crampons: A steel framework of spikes strapped to boots to provide traction on snow and ice.

Crevasse: A fissure or crack in a snow-field or glacier, often deep.

Crux: Main difficulty.

Exfoliating: peeling due to weathering.

Exposure: airiness, state of being exposed or open, as in unimpeded distance of a fall.

Gendarme: An isolated rock tower or pinnacle, frequently encountered along a ridge.

Glen: A small secluded valley

Glissade: The act of sliding down a steep snow-slope, either standing or seated; normally a voluntary manoeuvre.

Ice-axe: Wooden or metal shaft usually 2-3 feet long with an adze-shaped steel head at one end and a sharp spike at the other. Opposite the adze, the head is drawn to a point set with teeth. Used to stop a glissade, to facilitate travel on snow and ice and chop steps.

Massif: A central mountain mass. The dominating part of a mountain range.

Moraine: Rock debris transported and deposited by a glacier at its sides and front.

Rappel: Descending by sliding down a rope while controlling speed with friction.

Scree: Loose, broken rock at the foot of a cliff; slopes of debris caused by disintegration.

Self-arrest: Technique whereby one's ice-axe is used to stop a glissade.

Syncline: Trough-shaped fold in mountain strata.

Summit: Highest point of a mountain peak.

Talus: Same as scree. In mythology, Talus was a fearsome brute who did battle with rocks from his home in Crete.

Tarn: A small high-mountain lake typically occupying a glacially-scoured basin.

Thrust: A geological movement where continued folding of layers results in eventual shearing, thereby allowing the upper layer to slide onto and overlay the original rock. The break is known as a thrust fault; the overlying strata are a thrust sheet.

Traverse: To travel laterally without gaining elevation.

Park Administrative Offices

Kanaskis Country Office, Canmore	(403) 678-5508
Parks Canada Regional Office	(403) 292-4440

Information Centres

Waterton	(403) 859-2352
Elbow Valley	(403) 949-4261
Bow Valley Prov Park	(403) 673-3663
Barrier Lake Information Centre	(403) 673-3985
Kananaskis Lakes Visitor Centre	(403) 591-7222
Banff	(403) 762-4256
Banff (French language information)	(403) 762-4834
Lake Louise	(403) 522-3833
Yoho	(604) 343-6324
Columbia Icefields	(604) 761-7030
Jasper	(403) 852-6161

Travel Alberta

Travel Alberta (summer)	1-800 222-6501
(May to mid Oct)	(403) 678-5277
Field	(604) 343-6446

Weather Reports

Banff	(403) 762-2088
Jasper	(403) 852-3185

Reservations

Alpine Club of Canada Huts	(403) 678-3200
Banff National Park Huts	(403) 762-4256
Lake O'Hara Bus & Campground	(604) 343-6433
Canadian Alpine Centre Lake Louise	(403) 522-2200

Peaks by Degree of Difficulty

Alphabetical Index of Peaks

In an Emergency

In an emergency, contact
the Royal Canadian Mounted Police (RCMP) or
the nearest Ranger or Warden Office

RCMP Offices

Crowsnest	562-2867
Waterton (May - Oct)	859-2244
Waterton (Nov - Apr)	653-4932
Kananaskis	591-7707
Canmore	678-5516
Banff	762-2226
Lake Louise	522-3811
Field	343-6316
Jasper	852-4848

Park Ranger or Warden Offices

Waterton	859-2477
Kananaskis Country Emergency	591-7767
Elbow	949-3846
Banff	762-4506
Lake Louise	522-3866
Field	343-6324
Saskatchewan Crossing	761-7077
Sunwapta	852-6181
Columbia Icefields	761-7030
Poboktan Creek	852-5383
Jasper	852-6156